"Few chefs can communicate with equal measures of expertise and openheartedness like Camilla Wynne, who has seemingly made it her life's mission to share her love of fruit preservation with the world. And for that, we are so, so grateful. In the dazzling *Nature's Candy*, she has set her sights on creating and baking with candied fruit, a topic that may seem esoteric and peculiar to some, but to Camilla is a vast, scrumptious world brimming with possibility and joy."

NATASHA PICKOWICZ, **author of *More Than Cake***

"The only book you need for elevating seasonal fruits and vegetables into glistening jewels of flavor. Camilla offers insight into time-honored preserving methods with her own creative genius as a concise but thorough guide."

SARAH OWENS, **James Beard Award-winning author and baker**

"Camilla is a natural teacher, unmatched in her knowledge of preserving. She has an extraordinary talent for updating classical techniques for the modern kitchen. In *Nature's Candy* she has created an absolutely gorgeous, precious jewel-box of a book that will certainly pave the way for a truly triumphant renaissance of candied fruit everywhere. Yippee!"

NICOLA LAMB, **author of *Sift* and creator of Kitchen Projects**

"There is no better guide to the sweet, glistening, endlessly fascinating adventure that is candying fruit than Camilla Wynne. Her recipes are smart, instructive, and beyond fun, offering both an introduction to and deep dive in the ever colorful, transformative world of candied fruit. *Nature's Candy* is already a permanent staple on my shelves."

REBEKAH PEPPLER, **author of le SUD: *Recipes from Provence-Alpes-Côte d'Azur*, *Apéritif*, and *À Table***

"I've always found the idea of candying intimidating, but Camilla makes the process feel so straightforward and achievable. *Nature's Candy* will be one of the most used books in my kitchen and the bakery will be filled with candied fruits every season. Glorious, fruity heaven!"

ANNA HIGHAM, author of *The Last Bite*

NATURE'S CANDY

NATURE'S CANDY

Timeless and Inventive Recipes for Creating and Baking with Candied Fruit

Camilla Wynne

appetite
by RANDOM HOUSE

Appetite by Random House® and colophon are registered trademarks
of Penguin Random House LLC.

Library and Archives Canada Cataloguing in Publication is available upon request.
ISBN: 978-0-525-61268-1
eBook ISBN: 978-0-525-61269-8

Photography by Mickaël A. Bandassak
Food styling by Michelle Marek and Camilla Wynne
Book and cover design by Lisa Jager
Typeset by Terra Page

Printed in China

Published in Canada by Appetite by Random House®,
a division of Penguin Random House Canada Limited.
www.penguinrandomhouse.ca

10 9 8 7 6 5 4 3 2 1

appetite
by RANDOM HOUSE | Penguin
Random House
Canada

To Dorian, the sweetest one

"That something is difficult must be one more reason for us to do it."

RAINER MARIA RILKE

Table of Contents

Foreword

by Tim Mazurek

At a time when so many cookbooks are focused on the quick and practical, bending to our busy lives and endless obligations, Camilla Wynne is here to suggest (the audacity!) that we start spending our precious free time . . . candying fruit. Yes, candying fruit, the seemingly arcane and ancient method of fruit preservation. But that doesn't faze Camilla. She knows that life is about more than our basic needs and that sometimes pleasure needs to be pursued.

So along comes Camilla—probably wearing a ridiculously good outfit—to suggest, calmly, quietly, but with convincing force, that we consider the fruit.

If you're anything like me, your main exposure to candied fruit came at Christmastime when someone in your family made fruitcake. Invariably using the candied fruit in plastic tubs that appear out of nowhere in supermarkets every November and then disappear, unnoticed, early in the new year. Tubs full of unnatural but evocative colors that hint at flavors that they usually lack—though does anyone really know what a green cherry should taste like? The fruit is so insipid that it is easily overpowered by the heavy spicing of Auntie's cake and mostly provides something that can best be described as flair.

Camilla is here to save you from those tubs because, nostalgia aside, they're really not very good. She is also here to expand your use of candied fruit, to convince you it is worth your time and has all sorts of uses in your busy 21st-century kitchen. This isn't her first rodeo. Camilla's first two books championed the art of canning, a less forgotten but still uncommon kitchen task. She easily convinced many of us that it was worth our time to make our own jam, preserves, and pickles. She walked us through important things like avoiding botulism and somehow made it feel fun. She also suggested fresh flavor combinations (Mango and sea buckthorn jam, anyone?) that brought canning into the present day. Those first two books earned Camilla a legion of devout fans, myself included, who now spend their summers making jam and the rest of the year baking with it.

But I admit that even for me, a very serious home baker, candying fruit felt like a bridge too far. That was until I took a class with Camilla and pulled a glistening slice of pineapple from a jar of syrup that I had candied myself. Those pineapple slices were better than anything I could buy in a store, even in a fancy store. Well, maybe there is a fancy store in France that can do it that well, but I am not in France. Point being: the fruit you candy at home is full of life and flavor and is worth every effort you make!

I have found through the classes I have taken with Camilla that she is my ideal teacher: patient, curious, encouraging, and exacting. I have witnessed things going very wrong for classmates and Camilla isn't fazed. It can be saved! Or begun again. And she has a unique ability to translate her style of teaching into her books—into this book.

Using the methods Camilla lays out on these pages, you (just normal you!) will be able to take fruit and transform it into something magical, freezing it in time and amplifying its flavor. In an age of globalization, with fruits from all over the world filling the shelves year-round at your local green-grocer, this isn't necessary—but it sure is nice.

You'll be able to candy citrus peel, cherries, and even violets. And then, importantly, Camilla will give you scores of ideas for what to do with that candied fruit. If I haven't convinced you, you'll convince yourself when you take your first bite of her stollen pound cake (page 90) or quince and mascarpone cheesecake (page 83) and realize how candying fruit just upped your baking game. You'll soon be casually dropping the phrase "some fruit I candied" and people will respond, in shock: You made it? Let's be real, half of the pleasure that comes from baking is the showing off.

And that's what this is all about for Camilla: pleasure. Which is its own kind of need. Because it may be true that nobody needs to candy fruit, but that is obviously beside the point.

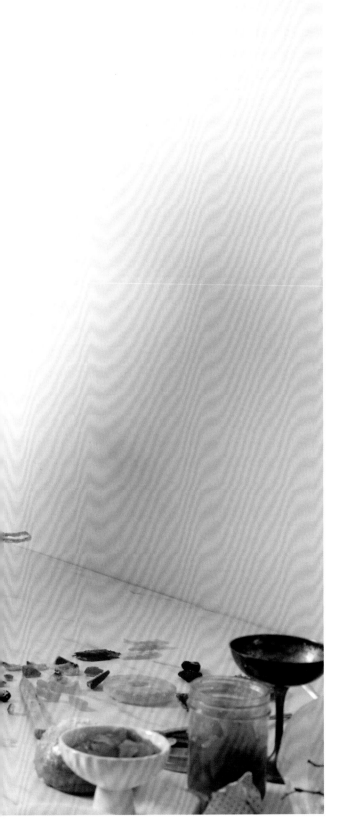

Introduction

I'm a child of the 80s, and in the Canadian Prairies (like elsewhere), that definitely involved malls. And, as a child, if I was allowed one treat on a trip to the mall, it wasn't going to be Cinnabon or Baskin-Robbins. I bee-lined it straight to the kiosk that mostly sold roasted nuts to grandpas and asked for a perfect, crystalline round of candied pineapple. How did they take a fruit I knew well and somehow transform it into candy?! Pineapple was good, but candied pineapple was a marvel.

I continue to love fruit more than almost anything else—my love of preserving springs from wanting to prolong the seasons of my favorites. Candy, on the other hand, I mostly feel ambivalent about. But candied fruit? I adore it, especially when it's made at home with beautiful fruit using just a few ingredients, sometimes with creative flavors, creating a jewel-like confection that still tastes like fruit.

Candied fruit, unfortunately, isn't very popular where I live in North America. Perhaps it's because supermarket candied cherries are bleached (something I still remember learning as a kid), which explains why they taste like nothing. Same goes for what passes as store-bought candied peel. And those bright pieces in much-maligned grocery-store fruitcake are candied turnip?! It's no wonder some people think they don't like candied fruit.

"Turns out I'm not the only one bewitched by glistening fruity jewels."

And yet! So many of our most cherished baked goods call for candied fruit in the ingredient list. These are classic recipes, often age-old traditions (page 5) from when fresh fruit wasn't as readily available out of season—stollen (page 90), nougat, Nesselrode pie (page 151), cannoli . . . the list goes on. Even an ice cream sundae or a Manhattan cocktail aren't complete without a candied cherry.

I've dabbled in candying my own fruit ever since pastry school, feeling quite all-powerful and armed with the skills to make my own *orangettes*, which I previously had to shell out money for at pastry shops. I'm mostly of British heritage, so making my own candied fruit for family classics like fruitcake and hot cross buns was a revelation that resulted in a much better baked good. I once even painstakingly candied a whole Victorian pineapple for a friend's birthday after being inspired by *À la Mère de Famille*, the cookbook by Julien Merceron. The pineapple still resides on her mantelpiece, like a specimen in formaldehyde, though of course its preservative is sugar.

It wasn't until I started teaching candied fruit techniques online during the pandemic that I really, really, really got into candied fruit. To be honest, I was shocked by the immense popularity of the workshop. Turns out I'm not the only one bewitched by glistening fruity jewels.

So allow me to be your Virgil. As in my workshop, I begin with a short history of fruit being turned into candy across the globe (page 5), followed by a look at the science behind sugar-preserved fruit (page 9). It may look like magic, but it's not! I then share some methods (page 23) that I've tested and tested to make candying as easy as possible—because I am a lazy Taurus who would rather read novels than measure syrup concentrations all day. It might take a little practice to figure out when a batch is perfectly candied, but so does almost everything worth doing. From there, you sample your candied fruit or glaze it, dip it in chocolate, or sugar it (page 60). Then bake with it!

The second section (page 70) contains delicious recipes illustrating some of the myriad ways you can incorporate candied fruit into your baking and confectionary. That said, nearly every recipe can stand on its own two feet even if you don't have time to candy your own fruit (page 13)! Of course, the recipes herein are informed by my prejudices and preferences, as in any cookbook. For instance, I don't like candied melon; melon, in my opinion, is just simply best consumed fresh. But if you want to make homemade *callisons*, this book will still teach you how to candy the melon. In fact, with this book you will be able to candy everything! Except limes. I still haven't figured those out.

So welcome to the sweet, fascinating world of candied fruit, one of the most ancient and gorgeous preservation methods in the universe.

A Very Brief History Lesson
Why, When & Where Did People Start Candying Fruit?

Though there isn't what you'd call a wealth of information out there about the history of candied fruit, there is some, and it is of course inextricably tied to the history of sugar.

Candied fruit's storied past begins with necessity. Like other fresh foods, fruit is subject to spoilage and has a limited lifespan, whether on the tree or your counter. Today many of us are accustomed to having access to fruits year-round at the grocery store on account of globalization and international shipping, with fruits imported from other parts of the world depending on their growing seasons. This availability is also thanks to scientific advances like refrigeration and controlled-atmosphere storage rooms, which essentially keep fruits like apples in hibernation. All of this technology is relatively new, though there have been steps along the way, such as apple storage rooms in Elizabethan England where the fruit was spread out in a single layer, as touching would cause them to spoil. Still, for most of our time on earth, humans have had to be satisfied with enjoying local fruits during short periods of seasonality.

In a bid to prolong the lifespan of their favorite fruits, people in both ancient China and ancient Rome found that storing them in a sealed vessel covered in honey or concentrated grape juice worked wonders. What's more, when they boiled the fruit in honey, one of the first candies was created. Fast-forward to the 10th century, when honey-preserved fruit recipes appeared in the first known Arabic cookbook. I have included my own version of a honied peel recipe on page 36.

Meanwhile, back around 500 BCE, India developed a method of making raw sugar from sugarcane, and then around 350 BCE, a method of refining it. A traveler to the region marveled at the "reeds that produce honey without bees."

Once sugar cultivation began in Persia around the 6th century—the land of quince, citron, and bitter oranges—candied fruit really got going. Arab and Persian immigrants brought a taste for sugar to China, inspiring a period of candied fruit mania in the 12th and 13th centuries. Concurrently, the Crusaders were bringing an appetite for sugar back to Europe.

By the end of the Middle Ages, sugar was still mostly a luxury for the rich. A ramp-up in production fueled by the horrors of slavery saw sugar replacing honey by the 16th century and becoming commonplace over the next

"Candied fruit's storied past begins with necessity."

hundred years, with the English developing the biggest sugar habit.

During this period, the English belief that eating raw fruit was unhealthy was still prevalent. They believed peaches provoked melancholy and that all fruit caused flatulence and simply rotted in the stomach! The sale of raw fruits was even banned during the plague year of 1569. By contrast, fruit cooked in sugar was considered healthy (ha!), but the candying didn't stop at fruits. Borage, sweet potato, sea holly, parsley roots, green walnuts, and lettuce stems were all subject to becoming suckets, as they called candied fruit at the time. Suckets could be dry or wet, and the latter were so popular as to merit their very own piece of cutlery: the sucket fork. With a fork on one end to retrieve the fruit and a spoon on the other end for the syrup, it was basically the original spork. Alas, most English households stopped candying their own fruit in the mid-19th century because of the convenience of increasingly affordable imports.

During the Middle Ages in France, candied fruits were known as *épices de chambre*, or bedroom spices, as they were eaten by royals in their chambers—in order to better enjoy them, of course. The area of Provence, where candied fruits have been produced by artisans since the 14th century, is still known for its superlative products.

In Italy, formal dinners once always ended with candied fruits, a custom I am eager to bring back in vogue. Many classic Italian desserts still popular today employ candied fruit, for instance, cassata, cannoli, and candied spumoni.

In Central and South America, due to the influence of Spanish and Portuguese colonists, candied fruit is a confectionary staple, with specialties including coconut-stuffed candied limes, piloncillo-candied pumpkin, and candied papaya.

In Vietnam, the celebration of Lunar New Year features a jewel-like assortment of candied fruits and vegetables, such as kumquats, winter melon, cassava, lotus seeds, and ginger. Around the world, candied fruits most often appear during holiday celebrations, as they can be either costly to buy or time-consuming to make.

In North America, it's a different story. While candied cherries and peel appear in the aisles of North American grocery stores—and you can see an abundance of fruitcake during the holidays—they are almost uniformly tasteless, leading most people to believe they don't like candied fruit at all. Mass production has led to bleached and brightly food-colored candied fruit, and the difference between this and a homemade or artisanal confection (page 13) is like night and day.

A Very Brief Science Lesson
How Does Candying Preserve Fruit & For How Long?

Fruits, like most other fresh foods, are prone to spoilage caused by bacteria, mold, and yeast. All those little pests need water to live, just like us. Luckily for them, fruits are 75% water! Fortunately, candying preserves fruits by replacing that water with sugar, vastly prolonging their lifespan.

That said, you can't just throw whole fruits into a concentrated sugar solution. They'd shrivel or burst. Instead, the sugar concentration must be increased gradually, slowly easing the fruit into a new state of being while keeping its original shape (and cell walls) intact. Sugar also keeps the fruit's color vibrant (or at least whatever wasn't lost in the initial simmer—some fruits shed a lot of color this way and are sometimes supplemented with food coloring).

The traditional method of candying fruit (at least in France) usually begins by briefly blanching fruit in water to soften it slightly and open the cell network, making it more amenable to soaking up syrup. Next, the fruit is soaked or simmered in a syrup whose density is increased little by little over a period of 3 to 4 weeks, which results in sugar taking the place of water in the cells of the fruit. Finally, the fruit is left to steep in the syrup for an additional month or two, ensuring its total penetration.

Scientists and confectioners use a measurement called Brix to describe the sugar concentration in an aqueous solution, 1 degree being equivalent to 1 g sucrose per 100 g liquid solution. Candied fruit is stable at room temperature at a sugar concentration of 75 Brix and is often finished with a final coating of concentrated sugar glaze as a protective shell. While artisans still produce beautiful fruit this way, industrial production now uses a vacuum process to speed things up.

But what of the home cook? Candying fruit in the manner of French artisans is not exactly a task to undertake at home. I can testify that when I've tried even a truncated version, I've ended up with a very syrup-sticky kitchen in spite of my best efforts, as well as a very detailed diary attempting to keep track of the multi-day process. And at the end of it all, I've ended up with crystallized fruit (page 11) every time. If you're not using a refractometer, a tool that measures the sugar concentration in a solution (like that 75 Brix I mentioned), know that it's difficult to replicate this process just using indications like boiling times or temperatures.

For this reason, I've long candied fruit using a quick shortcut method that I learned from the first *Tartine* cookbook. This Almost All-Purpose method (page 25) forgoes the blanching and gradual increases in sugar concentration in favor of quickly candying fruit in simple syrup. It takes only about 30 minutes and produces something delicious and useful. That said, the downside is that it can only be used on fruit sliced no thicker than about ¼ inch, as otherwise the sugar can't penetrate the fruit fully in such a short period of time. Additionally, because the finished product has a lower concentration of sugar (and therefore more water), it doesn't have the same shelf life. Fruit candied this way has a Brix closer to 60, which will still keep for ages if stored properly, but will never be as completely impervious to decay as the artisanal method. That said, less sugar tends to mean more fruit flavor!

The Tough Customers method (page 33), which is mainly used for candied citrus peel and sliced or diced ginger, builds on the Almost All-Purpose method with a pre-simmer to soften those fruits up first. They too can keep for a while if stored properly.

However, at a certain point I found myself wanting to replicate those gorgeous whole candied fruits I'd seen on display in Paris, so I came up with my Whole-ish method (page 28), which lands somewhere between the quick shortcut and artisanal methods. After blanching, the fruit is simmered briefly in syrup for 10 minutes per day, and increases in concentration each day. On average, it's 3 days, but it may need a few more days of simmering to cook off excess water depending on the fruit. Fruits candied this way should have a Brix of around 70. This means they're not totally bulletproof, but they will last longer than fruits candied with the Almost All-Purpose (page 25) or Tough Customers (page 33) methods, with the bonus that whole fruits and larger pieces can be treated this way.

HOW TO

Prevent Crystallization

Crystallized candied fruit (not to be mistaken with the Crystallization method on page 49) can look like it has bloomed with some unpleasant white substance or has grown stalagmites. Sucrose (aka table sugar) loves and is attractive to water, which leads it to draw water out of fruit—one step on the road to candying. The problem is sucrose loves itself more. Sucrose in solution (aka dissolved in water) would very much like to return to crystal formation, and it can happen when the sugar concentration in a solution is high (such as when candying fruit!), as there aren't enough water molecules to keep the sucrose molecules separated.

While certainly not the only pitfall on the road to perfectly candied fruit, crystallization is fairly easily avoided from the get-go by adding an ingredient to the syrup that will help disrupt the formation of sucrose crystals. In case this does happen, I have some troubleshooting tips to help on page 67.

Scientifically speaking, the best tool in the arsenal is an invert sugar, which bonds to the surface of sucrose crystals, impeding them from clustering. My preferred invert sugar is glucose syrup, but it's not readily available to home cooks (or if it is, it's stupidly expensive). Instead, I recommend inexpensive light corn syrup in most of my recipes, which is basically watered-down glucose and glucose-fructose with a little vanilla flavoring and salt.

However, there are plenty of places worldwide where corn syrup is not readily available either. Honey and golden syrup can work in a pinch, but because they alter the color and flavor of the finished product and are prone to caramelization, they aren't my first choice. Also, though honey generally stays in liquid form, we've all had a jar of it crystallize on us, which is just the thing it's meant to prevent here. And golden syrup is only a partially invert syrup, so not ideal.

You'll notice that some recipes call for adding acid to the sugar and water instead of an invert sugar. When heated, the acid should break the sucrose down into glucose and fructose, thus preventing crystallization. Unfortunately, I've never found the amounts to be very precise (a pinch or knife's tip is often called for), so I find the method far less reliable. This is why light corn syrup is the easiest to use.

Some Thoughts on Buying Quality Candied Fruit

The fact that you're reading this book likely means you want to make and bake with candied fruit. Great! However, sometimes you need a shortcut. Maybe you want to bake something that requires too many types of fruit to candy all at once, or a fruit that you can't find fresh—or perhaps you just don't have it in you to babysit a simmering bath of syrup this week. I get it.

That's where store-bought candied fruit comes in, the quality of which varies wildly. It ranges from bleached, dyed, and tasteless to whole glistening fruits that look like jewels and taste divine. In general, the more artisanal the product, the better it should be—as is usually the way. Fruit candied in smaller batches by skilled confectioners will always be preferable to mass-produced schlock, which I blame for people thinking they don't like candied fruit. Candied fruit sold in jars and preserved in syrup is usually a great option, whether it's English stem ginger or small Italian strawberries. Not only are they more versatile, but you get a delicious syrup to boot (see potential uses on page 27)!

Of course, typically, the better it is, the more you should expect to pay, at least in North America, where the choice tends to be cheap grocery-store tubs or imports from Europe. That said, if you're planning on baking with it, exquisite (and expensive) whole candied fruits are probably not the best choice. Actually, some commercial products are so good that I rarely bother to candy the same fruit at home. Amarena cherries are the best example. Richly flavored sour cherries preserved and jarred as perfect orbs in aromatic syrup, they're hard to beat. Even if I were able to buy these particularly well-suited cherries fresh, I would still probably buy them candied instead of making them myself. They are perfect and generally quite affordable (I even got a kilo jar at Costco at Christmas). To be honest, I also have a soft spot for bright red commercial maraschino cherries, for which I think there is a definite time and place (notably, sundaes).

If you don't live somewhere with an excellent candied fruit culture, since candied fruit traditions abound in countries across the globe, perhaps you'll be lucky enough to procure some on your travels. You can also ask someone more jet-set than you to bring some home. While I've never visited Vietnam or Mexico, I've had amazing candied fruit gifted to me by friends traveling to those countries. What a treat.

CAN

PART I

Thus We Begin
FAQ on Candying Fruit

So, you want to candy fruit . . . Here is some information to get you started on your candying journey. When in doubt, refer to the table on pages 56–57.

What kind of fruit can I candy?

Most fruits take well to candying, but certain methods tend to work better for certain fruits (more on that on page 23). Whatever the fruit, using slightly underripe will create the best texture. Overripe citrus can be tough, while softer fruits can easily disintegrate when overripe. Fruits that are very juicy are generally not the best candidates because so much water needs to be replaced with sugar; you'll find they shrink quite a bit.

Can you candy different fruits at once?

If you're looking to candy multiple fruits, you might think that doing them all at once is the move, but it will only work if they are all similarly sized and textured and will therefore cook at the same rate. You can combine soft fruits like cherries and strawberries, for instance, but you wouldn't want to pair either of them with quince. That said, I generally prefer to candy my fruits separately for the most precision, with the

exception of an orange, lemon, and grapefruit peel combo (page 33).

Can you candy canned or frozen fruits?

Yes, with caveats. On the plus side, they're accessible and save time, plus you don't need to precook when using my Whole-ish method (page 28), since they've already been exposed to heat from canning or lost water from freezing. That said, at least in my experience, they're never going to quite live up to the taste and texture of fresh candied fruit (as long as you're using excellent fresh fruit). If using frozen fruit, first thaw and drain before proceeding (you can use the liquid in place of some or all of the water, if you like). Frozen peels and ginger can be blanched from frozen according to the method on page 33, but you'll have to defrost them first if they aren't already cut to size.

What about candied vegetables?

Why stop at fruit? We regularly bake with vegetables like carrots, zucchini, winter squash, and beets, so why not candy them? Historically, people have candied vegetables as a lower-cost alternative to fruit, making mock candied ginger from bolted lettuce stalks or mock candied pineapple using zucchini and a little pineapple juice. Even now, a lot of cheap fruitcake actually uses cheap candied turnip in place of fruit! I think the error there is trying to pass off the vegetables for something else, which they likely can't quite emulate. Instead, we can candy vegetables to appreciate their unique flavors.

Winter melon, parsnips, carrots, pumpkin, fennel, and chili peppers all candy well. My friend Natasha Pickowicz has even candied mushrooms! Simply choose the Almost All-Purpose (page 25) or Whole-ish (page 28) method, according to the size of pieces you want to candy.

If you want ideas for using your candied vegetables, check out the Morning Glory Granola (page 179) and Chi's Spicy Strawberry Margarita Cookies (page 118). You could also make some stunning Mendiants (page 139) using candied vegetables!

Can you candy flowers?

Not the traditional way, but the Crystallization method will work (see page 49). Sturdy hibiscus flowers are the exception; they can be candied using the Almost All-Purpose method (page 25).

Which candying method should I choose?

You can use a few different methods to candy your fruit—whether you're looking for a quick simmer to use in a recipe or want to nurse a whole fig over a week to plump immortality. Choosing the method depends on the fruit itself—its texture and size—and

what you plan to do with the finished product. The table on pages 56–57 will help you decide which approach to take. While this is by no means an exhaustive list of fruits, it should get you started on your candied fruit journey. The more experience you have, the easier it will be to guess which approach will work best on a new fruit. And if it doesn't work out? Well, science experiments are fun too.

I'm baking something that calls for mixed candied fruit. Can I use any method?

In essence, yes. Ideally you just have a fridge full of different candied fruits already to draw upon, but if you're starting from scratch, stick to the standard candied methods that fit best for the fruit you have in mind: Almost All-Purpose (page 25), Whole-ish Candied Fruit (page 28), Candied Citrus Peel & Ginger (page 33), and/or Candied Taut-Skinned Berries & Their Ilk (page 39). The other methods, like candied fruit chips (page 40) or crystallization (page 49), result in such different textures, which aren't a good fit . . . and if you're feeling overwhelmed, you can always employ some high-quality store-bought candied fruit (page 13).

I need to finely chop, dice, or mince my candied fruit. Do I do that before I begin to candy?

No! Not unless you want to—but larger pieces tend to be more versatile. With the exception of ginger (page 35), you can chop your candied fruit as needed after it's been candied. That said, some fruit can be sliced or halved before you begin. See the table on pages 56–57 on how best to proceed.

Can I flavor my candied fruit?

You sure can. See page 26 for some ways you can get creative.

I've candied my fruit. What next?

Choose your own adventure. You can store it (page 59), dry it (page 59), finish it with a coating of glaze, sugar, or chocolate (page 60), or bake with it (page 70).

What if I want to transform my candied fruit into fun little shapes?

Bows, flowers, you name it, I have included some fun tips and tricks on pages 53–54. Each method is a bit different (some you embellish before you candy and some after), so read through first and plan accordingly.

Uh-oh, I think something went wrong. What do I do?

First, it happens; don't fret. Second, I've got you covered. Check out my troubleshooting tips on page 67.

Clockwise: candied jalapeños, lychees,
pear, hibiscus, and pineapple

Methods

There are many methods for candying fruit, but I have found that the following make for the best final product with the least amount of trouble. I have learned them over the years from pastry chefs, confectioners, and cookbooks, then tested and retested to simplify them as much as possible.

When I teach my candied fruit class, I always start with my Almost All-Purpose method (page 25). It's quick and, as the title suggests, is almost all-purpose. For larger pieces of fruit, turn to the Whole-ish method (page 28). It takes at least 4 days, so plan ahead. Citrus peel and ginger, due to their texture, have their own method, on page 33—the honied peel version (page 36) is fun too.

For thinly sliced fruit, check out Candied Fruit Chips (page 40)—they make gorgeous decor for your desserts. Have fragile fruit? Gently ply them with syrup using my Candied Fruit Lite method (page 43). For especially shiny and fancy-looking fruit, the Glacé Fruits & Nuts method (page 47) is the one to try. Craving candied nuts or coconut? I share the simplest method I know on page 44. And lastly, if you want to make a garnish or décor without preserving the fruit, you can crystallize (page 49) it in a variety of ways.

If you aren't sure where to turn, check out the table on pages 56–57.

Top to Bottom: Candied carrot, kiwi, kumquat, quince, and clementine

Almost All-Purpose
Candied Fruit
aka The Speediest Method for Small Pieces

If you're new to candying, start here. I learned this quick method from the excellent book *Tartine* by Elisabeth Prueitt and Chad Robertson. It has its limits, in that it will only work or relatively small pieces of fruit (if you want to candy a whole fruit or large pieces using a method closer to that of an artisan confectioner, head to page 28). It also won't make a product that is completely shelf-stable, but you can't beat it for speed! The final product works beautifully for baking with or serving on its own.

Only use fruit with a strong cell structure that can handle a hearty simmer (not raspberries, for instance; the best method for them is on page 43). Good candidates include pineapples, kiwis, quinces, pears, cherries, apple peels, and thin-skinned citrus like clementines and kumquats (see page 33 for candying thicker-skinned citrus). For a full list of which methods are best for the fruit you have, see the table on pages 56–57.

Because only you know how much fruit you want to candy, I prefer to use ratios. The ratio for the syrup is 1:1 water to sugar by cup, so make as much or as little as you need, depending on how much fruit you have. While I generally prefer to measure by weight, what's important here is that there is enough syrup to cover the fruit. For each cup of prepared fruit, you'll need about 190 mL (¾ cup) water, 150 g (¾ cup) sugar, and 1 tablespoon glucose or light corn syrup.

To prepare the fruit, peel, core if necessary, and slice about ¼ inch thick. Cherries should be halved and pitted. Clementines can be cut into six to eight wedges. Kumquats can be sliced or quartered.

To candy the fruit, in a medium saucepan, bring the water, sugar, and glucose to a boil over high heat, stirring occasionally to dissolve the sugar. Add the fruit and immediately reduce the heat to a gentle simmer. Cook until the fruit is uniformly glossy and translucent, anywhere from 15 to 45 minutes depending on the fruit. Soft fruits like cherries, for instance, will take less time, while dense fruits like quinces will take the longest. Remove from the heat and allow to cool completely in the syrup at room temperature, preferably overnight, before storing, drying, or finishing (pages 59–60).

HOW TO

Get Creative with Flavorings from Verjus to Spices

While candied fruit on its own is a beautiful thing (obviously), sometimes you want to embellish and flex your flavor muscle. There are a number of easy ways to imbue your candied fruit with different flavors, no matter the method you choose. Whether adding a single accent note or replicating a favorite cocktail, dessert, or snack—like fresh pineapple sprinkled with chili, salt, and sugar—the trick is to be modest when adding flavorings. Taste as you go. You can usually add more flavor, but you can never take it away. Here are some ideas.

SWAP SOME SUGAR: Swap out up to half of the granulated sugar in the syrup for brown sugar, be it golden or muscovado, for a caramel hue and rich flavor. (Swapping more than half will eclipse the fruit flavor with a molasses flavor from those darker sugars and potentially make it hard to judge doneness.)

ADD WHOLE SPICES TO THE SYRUP: Warm spices like cinnamon, star anise, cloves, allspice, cardamom, and mace all classically pair well with sugar and fruit, but try experimenting with more savory players like coriander, pepper, chili, fennel, juniper, and saffron. Try dry-toasting them first to release extra flavor—just a few minutes in a dry pan over medium heat, stirring to make sure they don't burn. Oh, and a split, scraped vanilla bean is never a bad idea.

ADD FRESH OR DRIED HERBS AND FLOWERS: Fresh or dried herbs and flowers can be used like spices, although I generally favor fresh if available. Makrut lime leaves, curry leaves, rosemary, chamomile, basil, verbena, lavender, and hibiscus all work well.

ADD TEA LEAVES OR COFFEE BEANS: These can be added either directly into the syrup or steeped using a tea ball during cooking. Both work, but steeping will give you better control over the finished product, allowing you to easily remove it if on the verge of becoming too strong or bitter. Espresso powder is also a good option!

BRING ON THE ACID: With a confection as sweet as candied fruit, some acid is always welcome to balance the flavor. While I often add citric acid to my finishing sugar, you can also add vinegar (fruit vinegar, in particular, and any kind, as long as it tastes good), sour citrus juice, or verjus to the candying syrup for an added layer. Add a few glugs once the fruit is done cooking, then let it sit overnight at room temperature before storing.

TRY ADDING ALCOHOL: Fortified wines and aperitifs can be added at the beginning of cooking, though anything very dark may make it difficult to judge doneness. Add stronger spirits like rum, whisky, and gin, to taste, at the end of cooking.

FINISH IT: Finish the candied fruit, dried until just tacky, with flavored sugar (page 62).

Great Combinations

- Cherries with vanilla bean, cinnamon, and brandy
- Clementine wedges with brown sugar, cinnamon, cloves, allspice, and dark rum
- Grapefruit peel with Campari, rolled in sour Campari sugar
- Pineapple with lime zest, coriander, arbol chili, and mezcal, rolled in sweet, salty, and spicy sugar blend
- Pumpkin with panela, espresso powder, cinnamon, cloves, and star anise (pumpkin spice latte vibes)
- Cherry tomatoes with vanilla bean, rolled in basil sugar
- Fennel with lemon zest and pastis

Sweet Elixir! Save the Syrup

While some might see the syrup as simply a by-product of candied fruit, I see it as LIQUID GOLD. Seriously, people, bottle and sell this stuff for a high price. Beyond the baking recipes in this book that use candied fruit syrup, there are so many things you can do with it. Some ideas:

- As a soak to moisten layers of cake, such as my Quince, Chestnut & Chocolate Layer Cake (page 100)
- To sweeten lemonade or iced tea
- In fancy coffee drinks (candied pumpkin syrup works especially well in pumpkin spice lattes for obvious reasons)
- In cocktails or mocktails in place of simple syrup
- In savory recipes that need a little sweet note (I like using it as a glaze for root vegetables or adding it to vinaigrettes or barbecue sauces)
- Once reduced until slightly thickened, to glaze tarts or pound cakes . . . or ham
- As a sub for liquid sweetener in anything—experiment!

Whole-ish Candied Fruit

aka Level Up with a Slightly More Laborious Method

The Almost All-Purpose method (page 25) is wonderful and quick for candying fruit to bake with or even for candy boxes, but if you want to candy larger pieces of fruit similar to what you'd see in the windows of Provence confectioners, you'll need to do it over a few days, allowing the syrup to slowly permeate the flesh. I'm talking glossy whole figs, thick Seville orange slices to dip in chocolate, marrons glacés, plump kumquats, and thick papaya spears— even whole Victorian pineapples or small squash. For a full list, see the table on pages 56–57. This method is not really more work; it just takes more time, and for a few days it monopolizes a pot that you might otherwise like to use to steam some vegetables.

Day 1: First you'll need to simmer the fruit gently to make its membranes more permeable and amenable to receiving the sugar. Fruit with skin (like kumquats, figs, or cherries) should be pricked all over with a skewer first. Place the fruit in a heavy-bottomed pot and cover with water. (For large slices of citrus or pineapple, I prefer to use a wide, shallow pan to keep them in a single layer as much as possible.)

Bring just to a boil over medium-high heat, then reduce the heat to a gentle simmer. Cook until heated through and slightly softened—delicate fruits like whole strawberries need only 5 minutes, but most fruits will take 10 minutes (although very firm pieces, like orange slices or ginger, will need about 30 minutes).

Remove from the heat and carefully drain the water, then rinse the sides of the pot under cold water to let it cool. Place the pot

with the drained fruit on a tared (zeroed) scale and add enough water to cover, noting the weight (and writing it down to reference later). Add one-third of the original weight of water in sugar and bring to a boil over medium-high heat. Reduce the heat to a simmer and cook for 10 minutes (or 5 for fragile fruits). Remove from the heat, cover, and let sit at room temperature overnight.

Day 2: The next day, add the same amount of sugar again (one-third of the weight of the water). Bring to a boil over medium-high, then reduce the heat to a simmer and cook for 10 minutes (or 5 minutes for fragile fruits). Remove from the heat, cover, and let sit at room temperature overnight.

Day 3: The next day, add the same amount of sugar for the last time, along with ½ tablespoon glucose or light corn syrup

continued

Day One

Day Two

Day Three

Day Four

Left to Right, Top to Bottom:
Candied clementine, cactus pear,
papaya, pear, fig, kumquat,
apricot, Seville orange, donut
peach, pineapple, sour cherry,
and strawberry

per 100 g water you noted in Day 1. Bring to a boil over medium-high heat, then reduce the heat to a simmer and cook for 10 minutes (or 5 minutes for fragile fruits). Remove from the heat, cover, and let sit overnight.

Day 4 (or More): The next day, check your fruit. It might be ready! You're looking for glossy, plump, and translucent fruit with no undercooked patches, surrounded by a moderately viscous syrup. If it looks like it isn't quite there yet, not to worry—many fruits will need more time, especially larger pieces or denser-fleshed fruits such as large figs or whole clementines. Repeat the 5- to 10-minute simmering process (but without adding any more sugar) and rest at room temperature overnight every day until you are satisfied. I've never gone past a week.

When ready, store, dry, or finish (pages 59–60).

HOW TO

Pretreat for Sturdier Shapes

Firm fruit like whole clementines and pears will keep their shape well when candied using the Whole-ish method (page 28), but more tender fruits like figs and kumquats tend to collapse a bit when dried. This is, however, largely preventable. If you want to candy fruit that really doesn't hold its shape, a bath in calcium hydroxide will help significantly.

Calcium hydroxide—aka pickling lime or slaked lime—is a chemical with many uses ranging from culinary to medical to sewage treatment to paper production. For this reason, it's important to always use *food-grade calcium hydroxide*. It can be found sold with canning supplies (even though it's no longer considered safe for use in pickling due to an increased risk of botulism because of its really high pH) or at specialty grocers, particularly Latin or Mediterranean. Often used for nixtamalization to make tortillas, it's also commonly used to pretreat fruit for candying in Central and South American countries. It's used in Greek spoon sweets, as well, to keep the fruit plump and shapely. Calcium binds to pectin in the fruit, making it firmer.

TO PRETREAT FRUIT, in a glass or stainless-steel bowl, mix 2 tablespoons calcium hydroxide per liter of cold water (there should be enough liquid to completely submerge the fruit). Carefully add the fruit and soak for a minimum of 6 hours if you're in a rush, and up to 24—more is better. Drain, then rinse very thoroughly before proceeding with the recipe.

NOTE *EMPLOY CAUTION when using calcium hydroxide. With a pH of 12, it's very caustic and can severely irritate and burn the skin and eyes, and it should not be inhaled or ingested. Be careful when handling and be sure to wash your hands immediately afterward. It probably goes without saying that it should be kept out of reach of children and pets.*

Candied Citrus Peel & Ginger

aka The Method for Tough Customers

Citrus peel and ginger are candied fruit stalwarts that bring bitter and spicy complexity, respectively, to the table. On account of their texture, however, a slightly different approach is required, but it's as simple as adding a first step of simmering in water to soften them up.

Unlike many candied peel and ginger recipes, this method doesn't call for multiple boiling-water changes, the idea behind which is to eliminate strong flavors. As a lover of all things bitter and spicy, I'm not much concerned with trying to wrest what is essentially the character out of the candy. In this method, the peel or ginger is simply simmered until tender to prepare for candying. I think you'll find that the sugar does much to balance those flavors so that they're intriguing to the taste buds rather than overwhelming. The one exception to this is bergamot, a citrus fruit with such strong oils (you'll recognize the flavor from Earl Grey tea) that it must have its water changed at least three times during cooking.

This method works well for the majority of citrus fruits, such as oranges, lemons, and grapefruits, in their many varieties (though thin-skinned citrus, such as clementines, can simply be candied using the Almost All-Purpose method on page 25). To candy thick slices of citrus, see page 25. The exception here is limes, which become tough and unpleasantly chewy no matter the method (and I've tried many). If in doubt, check out the table on pages 56–57 for which method works best for your fruit.

As for ginger, young ginger is the best for candying, but unfortunately not easy to find. Check your local farmer's market in the fall to find the beautiful, tender specimens. A well-stocked Asian grocery store or natural foods store might have it as well (and make tea with the leaves if they come attached!). If you can't find it, however, you can make perfectly nice homemade candied ginger with the standard stuff at the grocery store.

To prep the citrus peel, using a small serrated knife, cut the top and bottom of the fruit just enough to expose the flesh. Stand it up on its bottom, then vertically cut swaths of peel off the fruit, leaving just a little flesh clinging on. The clinging flesh will have a tender, jelly-like texture when candied. The denuded fruit may now be used to candy citrus supremes (page 43) or make citrus wheels or juice. I like to leave the peel in large pieces like this because it gives me options for how to use it later on, but if you know you want to make *orangettes*, for instance, you can cut the pieces into strips right away.

continued

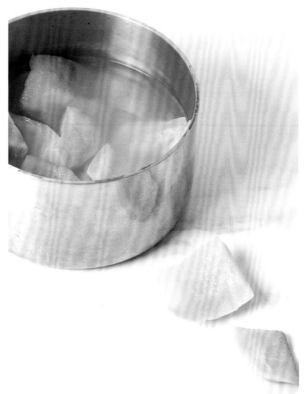

Alternatively, if you want to candy peels left over from juicing, simply scrape out the clinging, spent membranes, either by hand or with the help of a spoon, then cut the shells in half before proceeding.

To candy whole hollowed-out orange shells for Frozen Yogurt Candied Orange with Aperol Granita (page 167) or some other such use, cut the top ½ inch or so off the oranges so the flesh is exposed. Use a mini serrated knife or a paring knife to carefully cut between the peel and the flesh, removing the insides while keeping the shell intact (reserving flesh). Proceed as directed.

To prep the ginger, begin peeling the ginger by scraping off the peel with a metal spoon. Slice the ginger into ¼-inch-thick coins, or, if you know you want it diced, you can dice it now. (If you want to candy larger chunks of ginger, as for stem ginger, see page 28.)

To candy, put the prepared peel or ginger into a pot and cover with at least 2 inches of water. Bring to a boil over high heat, then simmer until tender. For peels, no uncooked white pith should be visible (some peel will have little white dots, which is fine). This will take anywhere from 30 to 45 minutes depending on the fruit (thicker peels such as pomelo will take longest). For young ginger, this should take about 30 minutes; for standard ginger, it should take up to 45 minutes. Drain and set aside. If you want spicier ginger, reserve the water to use in the syrup, or save it to drink as ginger tea.

In the same pot, combine equal parts sugar and water (by weight), adding 1 tablespoon glucose or light corn syrup per 250 g (1¼ cups) sugar. (For each cup of prepared peel or ginger, you'll need about 250 g/1 cup water and 250 g/1¼ cups sugar.)

Bring to a boil over high heat, then add the peel or ginger. Reduce the heat to medium and simmer gently, stirring occasionally, until shiny, translucent, and evenly cooked. The syrup will slightly thicken to a consistency somewhere between maple syrup and runny honey, but nothing more. This should take 1 to 2 hours, and you may need to reduce the heat progressively over that time to prevent it from boiling vigorously.

Remove from the heat and allow to cool completely in the syrup at room temperature, preferably overnight, before storing, drying, or finishing (pages 59–60).

HOW TO

Make Honied Peel

urious about the original method of candying fruit (page 5), which used honey, I gave it a try after finding a recipe for "Honied Peel" in an old Nabob Coffee recipe booklet of my grandmother's. It was the kind of short, vague paragraph of a recipe characteristic of vintage cookbooks, but with a little guesswork I nailed it (I think). The fruit came out glossy, translucent, and gorgeous. Unless you own an apiary, however, this isn't a thrifty recipe, calling for over a cup of honey (preferably a neutral-flavored local liquid honey) per orange (though you could use any citrus). But even if I were rich, it wouldn't be my personal first choice simply because the flavor of honey, while delicious, is so strong that I find it eclipses that of the fruit. If you're looking for alternatives to sugar, however, this might be just the ticket.

DAY 1: A baking soda soak is the first step in the process to help tenderize the peel. Combine 1 teaspoon baking soda per liter (4 cups) of water in a nonreactive bowl or measuring cup. This method works best using precut strips of peel, so juice your oranges, use a spoon to scrape out the membranes, and cut into ¼-inch strips. Add the strips to the baking soda solution and weigh them down with a plate or bowl to keep them submerged. Let stand at room temperature overnight.

DAY 2: Drain the peel, transfer to a pot, and cover with fresh water. Bring to a boil over high heat, then reduce the heat to a simmer. Cook until tender, about 30 minutes. Drain.

In a bowl or large measuring cup, prepare a weak honey solution by combining 1 part honey to 4 parts warm water by weight, stirring to dissolve the honey. Add the peels and weigh them down with a plate or bowl to submerge. Let stand at room temperature overnight.

DAY 3: Drain the peel and transfer to a pot. Add enough honey to cover the peel and bring to a simmer over medium heat. Reduce the heat to medium-low and simmer until the peel is glossy and translucent, 30 minutes to 1 hour. This mixture needs to cook on a lower heat than candied peel in sugar syrup, so keep a close eye on it, reducing the heat as needed to keep at a low simmer. Cover the pot and let cool at room temperature before storing, drying, or finishing (pages 59–60).

Candied Taut-Skinned Berries
& Their Ilk
aka The Pressurized Orbs Method

Small fruit with taut skins, such as cranberries, goldenberries, gooseberries, blueberries, and even cherry tomatoes, can't be candied by simmering in syrup. They are prone to exploding as the water inside the fruit expands and tears the skin.

Instead, I use a method I learned from Montreal pastry chef David Courteau (who is also a brilliant photographer and ceramicist—I'm very jealous). He very gently poaches the fruits, then shocks them in an ice bath to stop the cooking, drains, and steeps them in a cold simple syrup that seeps in over the course of a week. Brilliant. Check the table on pages 56–57 for the fruits that work best with this method. Note: You will need a thermometer.

To candy berries and their ilk, prepare the simple syrup (page 197) and let cool in the pot in the refrigerator. Make sure you have enough cold simple syrup on hand to cover the fruit (you'll need about half the volume of the jar you plan to put them in).

Pierce the bottom of each berry with a skewer. Place them in a pot and cover with cold water. Heat over medium heat until the water reaches 176°F (80°C). Meanwhile, prepare an ice water bath.

Immediately drain the berries and transfer to the ice water bath to stop the cooking process.

Transfer the berries to a jar and cover completely with the cold simple syrup. Place in the refrigerator for at least 1 week before finishing (page 60). They will keep in the refrigerator for at least 2 months but can be dried for longer storage (see page 59).

Candied Fruit Chips

aka 2D Translucent Cross–Sections

These ultra-thin fruit cross-sections can look almost transparent, making them gorgeous décor for pastries and desserts like Pear, Hazelnut & Caramel Layer Cake (page 97) or Quince & Mascarpone Cheesecake (page 83). Pears and quinces are the fruits I use most often with this method. Apples, Asian pears, pineapples, firm persimmons, and even strawberries and rhubarb also work well. See the table on pages 56–57 for a full list.

For every fruit of your choice (such as one pear), you'll need 200 g (1 cup) sugar, ½ teaspoon citric acid or 2 tablespoons lemon juice, and 250 mL (1 cup) water.

To begin, in a medium pot, combine the sugar and citric acid with the water and bring to a boil over medium-high heat.

Meanwhile, using a mandoline or a very sharp knife, vertically slice the fruit into $1/16$-inch-thick pieces.

When the syrup comes to a boil, reduce the heat to medium-low and add the fruit slices one at a time, submerging each one. Let simmer for 1 to 2 minutes. (If using more fragile fruit like strawberries or rhubarb, simply add to the pot and turn off the heat immediately. For firmer fruit like quince, simmer until pink and slightly softened, 15 to 30 minutes.) Remove from the heat, cover, and let sit at room temperature for at least 1 hour or up to overnight.

The tender, thin slices can be used now or stored in the syrup in an airtight container for at least 2 weeks in the refrigerator.

To make the candied fruit chips, have a food dehydrator close at hand or preheat the oven to 175°F (80°C) and line a baking sheet with a silicone mat or parchment paper.

Remove the slices from the syrup, shake off any excess syrup, and lay the slices on the food dehydrator trays or the prepared baking sheet. Dry for 1½ to 3 hours, until dry but not brittle and still slightly tacky. (If using the oven, check at 45 minutes to ensure they aren't overcooking.)

Let cool completely. Use immediately or store between layers of parchment or waxed paper in an airtight container for up to 1 month.

NOTE *Humidity is not the friend of fruit chips. If you have any silica packets, add them to the storage container to prolong the fruit chips' lifespan. When using fruit chips to decorate anything moist, like a cake, wait until the last minute if you want them to hold their shape!*

Candied Fruit Lite

aka Plying Fragile Fruits Gently with Syrup

What of the fragile fruits that would fall to absolute pieces when simmered in hot syrup? Raspberries, rhubarb, or citrus supremes left over from candying peel, to name a few (see the table on pages 56–57 for other fruits), can't quite be candied, but you can gently ply them with simple syrup. They won't last as long as regular candied fruit, but their lifespan will be prolonged with a week or two in syrup, or much longer if dried per the instructions on page 59. Unlike regular dried fruit, dried Candied Fruit Lite will be shiny, retain its color, and have a nice pliable texture.

As with the other candied fruit recipes, there's a great opportunity to add flavor here by infusing the syrup with any of the flavors listed on page 27. Grapefruit supremes in Campari syrup are amazing, especially when dried. Same goes for slender rhubarb batons.

To lightly candy, prepare the simple syrup (page 197). Place the fruit in a resealable container without leaving a lot of headspace. Bring enough simple syrup to cover the fruit (generally half the volume of the container) to a boil and pour over the fruit. Cover and cool to room temperature for 24 hours before storing in the refrigerator for about a week or drying (page 59).

Candied Nuts & Coconut

*aka Candying & Toasting Simultaneously
for a Sparkling & Crunchy Finish*

There are plenty of methods for candying nuts, but the one I use most regularly (learned back in my Montreal restaurant days) is the simplest one I know. Nuts (or fresh sliced coconut) are just tossed with simple syrup and then sugar, making a sandy coating that dries out in the oven while the nuts simultaneously toast. The result is sparkling, sweet, and crunchy. They're good as is, but you can add another layer by using flavored simple syrup or adding flavorings with the sugar, such as spices, salt, citrus zest, or ground espresso (see page 62 for some other ideas). I particularly like peanuts with a little flaky salt and espresso, or pecans with maple sugar.

To begin, preheat the oven to 350°F (175°C). Line a rimmed baking sheet with parchment paper or a silicone mat. Toss thinly sliced fresh coconut or raw nuts with just enough simple syrup (page 197) to moisten (be very modest, then add more if needed). Throw in a handful of sugar and toss to coat. The simple syrup should cause the sugar to adhere all over.

Spread in a single layer on the prepared pan. Bake for 10 to 12 minutes, until lightly toasted and dry.

Allow to cool completely before storing in an airtight container at room temperature. They will keep for at least 1 month.

Glacé Fruits & Nuts

aka A Quip Dip to Create a Luxurious-Looking Sugar Shell

Fresh fruit dipped in a shiny, shattering coating of sugar would be considered an antiquated dessert in North America, the stuff of vintage cookbooks. Funny, since that's pretty much what a candy apple is, just with a little added food coloring. Elsewhere in the world, however, it's a popular street food—just swap the silver platter for a skewer. *Tanghulu*, popular in northern China, uses hawthorn, while in Korea, *ddalgi satang* translates to "strawberry hard candy" (though the same technique is used on many different fruits). When dried fruits or nuts sandwiched with marzipan are given this treatment, they're known in France as *fruits déguisés*, or disguised fruits.

Whatever they're called, fruits (or nuts) that take a quick dip in a hard-crack syrup look extremely fancy. Grapes (in clusters or skewered), strawberries, kumquats, peeled clementines, and figs are all good candidates as their edible skin will prevent moisture from softening the sugar shell. And if you'd like to make them even fancier, swirl some edible glitter into the syrup right before dipping. You can also make caramel-dipped fruits by heating the syrup to a higher temperature. Use this method to make the caramel-coated hazelnuts for the Pear, Hazelnut & Caramel Layer Cake (page 97).

For fruits déguisés, flavor some marzipan by kneading in liqueur, zest, espresso powder, and/or spices, then stuff into a slit-open dried apricot, fig, prune, or date, or else sandwich between two whole walnuts or pecans. In fact, hawthorn are often hollowed out and filled with red bean paste in tanghulu, so consider stuffing fresh fruit as well!

For every 500 g (volume depends on surface area) of fruit, you'll need 400 g (2 cups) sugar, 125 mL (½ cup) water, 1 tablespoon light corn syrup, and ⅛ teaspoon cream of tartar.

To begin, line a baking sheet with parchment paper or a silicone mat. You must act quickly, so have clean, dry fruit close at hand along with a wooden skewer or oiled fork for dipping (a toothpick can also work for small fruits and nuts like grapes or hazelnuts). Prepare an ice bath that's large enough to place the bottom of the pot in.

In a medium pot over medium-high heat, combine the sugar, water, corn syrup, and cream of tartar. Bring to a hard boil, stirring occasionally to dissolve the sugar. Continue boiling until the mixture reaches 300°F (150°C) (or 340°F/170°C for caramel). Immediately plunge the bottom of the pot into the ice bath to halt cooking.

Quickly (and carefully) dip the fruit into the syrup to coat, then place on the prepared baking sheet to set. If the syrup begins to stiffen, rewarm over medium-low heat and gently stir.

Glacé fruits should be eaten the same day they are made, preferably within an hour or two.

Crystallization

aka Sugared Things That Look Candied & Sparkle

While the result of this method isn't technically candied (unless we're talking delicate flowers and leaves), this easy but impressive method makes fruits sparkle like frosted jewels. Fruits prepared this way make for stunning cake décor or a beautiful dessert garnish. That said, this treatment in no way preserves fruits, so after they dry overnight, they should be used as soon as possible. The exception to this rule is delicate edible flowers and leaves, such as violets, roses, pansies, nasturtiums, mint, and lemon balm, which are so thin that they will dry completely overnight and can be stored in an airtight container for at least a month. Use regular granulated sugar for a super-sparkly effect and superfine sugar for a subtler frosted look.

Egg White Method: You'll need a small food-safe paintbrush, a shallow bowl of sugar, a wire rack set over a rimmed baking sheet, and a small bowl of egg white. To be honest, I usually use fresh egg white, but if you want to be very cautious, you can use pasteurized egg white from a carton.

Brush the egg white all over the part of the fruit you want to sparkle, then dip the fruit into the sugar to coat. Transfer to the prepared wire rack and let dry for at least a few hours and up to overnight.

Gum Arabic Method: Gum arabic is certainly less readily available than egg whites, but I do find it gives a better result. You'll also want to use this for vegans or anyone with an egg allergy. Just mix the powder with a little water (or use rosewater or orange flower water for extra flavor) to get an egg white consistency, then proceed as above.

continued

Candied Flowers with Real Longevity:
Crystallized candied flowers and leaves last a while, but if you really want their color and shape to stay vibrant indefinitely, you'll need to do a little more work. Crystallize the flowers using the egg white or gum arabic methods on the previous page and let dry for 24 hours.

After they're dry, place them in a shallow bowl or pan and cover with cold 2:1 sugar syrup (a syrup made with double the weight of sugar to water; see the Variation on page 197). Cover the pan with plastic wrap and let sit 12 hours, after which time the petals should be covered in hard sugar crystals (if they aren't, check again in a few more hours). Set a wire rack over a rimmed baking sheet. Carefully drain the flowers and let dry completely on the wire rack before storing in an airtight container indefinitely.

In artisanal production, this process is made easier by using a *candissoire*, a container with a fitted rack that lets you easily lower the flowers into the syrup in a single layer and then drain the syrup from the bottom. I've made a DIY version by setting the rack from my air fryer inside a baking pan. This makes it easier to protect the delicate petals, as you can simply lift them out of the syrup using the rack.

HOW TO

Shape Your Candied Jewels

The natural shapes of fruits are certainly beautiful, but at times you may want to embellish. With the help of a knife or a set of cutters, it's possible to transform candied fruit into delightful shapes. They all have slightly different methods—some you shape before you candy and some after—so prepare accordingly if you know you want to make a certain shape. These are some of my favorites, but perhaps you'll be inspired to create your own unique shapes.

Bows

I am a real bow lover, whether for fashion or cakes. Bronwen Wyatt, my friend and absolutely brilliant cake maker (and so much more—she's really a star), came up with a genius way to make citrus peel bows, which I've reproduced here with her permission. Use a channel knife to remove a long, thin spiral of peel from a citrus fruit (it works best with more tender varieties like Meyer lemons), then candy directly in simple syrup (page 167). Drain and tie the peel into a beautiful bow before drying (page 53).

Another intelligent Internet friend and pastry goddess, Catherine Roberge, makes rhubarb bows. Use a sharp knife to slice long

continued

strips of rhubarb as thinly as possible, then steep overnight in warm simple syrup (see Candied Fruit Lite, page 43). Drain. Tie into bows and dry (page 53) before rolling in sugar for extra sparkle.

Flowers

Kumquat flowers are an ingenious technique popular in both Vietnam and China. Before candying, cut six lengthwise slits in the fruit from top to tail, nearly to the center. Once they are done candying (use the Almost All-Purpose method on page 25), press together the top and bottom so the peel resembles petals.

Another great method to make candied peel flowers comes from my dear friend, pastry chef Michelle Marek. She uses small flower-shaped fondant cutters on drained candied peel (orange, grapefruit, lemon—whatever!), then dries them to decorate cakes like her sublime Apricot & Orange Roll Cake (page 93).

Freestyle

There's no need to stop at bows and flowers. You could use an aspic or cookie cutter set (or even a knife; just be careful) to make whatever shapes you like—hearts or letters come to mind. This is most applicable to the Almost All-Purpose (page 25) and Candied Citrus Peel & Ginger (page 33) methods; just be sure to shape them after you candy.

The Best Method(s)
to Candy Each Fruit

LEGEND	
● Almost All-Purpose Candied Fruit (page 25)	● Candied Fruit Chips (page 40)
● Whole-ish Candied Fruit (page 28)	● Candied Fruit Lite (page 43)
○ Candied Citrus Peel & Ginger aka Tough Customers (page 33)	○ Candied Nuts & Coconut (page 44)
● Candied Taut-Skinned Berries & Their Ilk aka Pressurized Orbs (page 39)	● Glacé Fruits & Nuts (page 47)
	● Crystallization (page 49)

APPLES	● (peel) ● (thinly sliced)
APRICOTS	● (halved or whole)
BLUEBERRIES	● (whole)
CACTUS PEARS	● (sliced) ● (halved or whole)
CHERRIES	● (halved) ● (whole)
CHESTNUTS	● (best for whole chestnuts) ○ (this can work too for whole chestnuts) *(Note: Use cooked, vacuum-sealed chestnuts to avoid arduous peeling and parcooking.)*
CITRUS **THICK-SKINNED** **(E.G., CITRON,** **ORANGES, LEMONS,** **GRAPEFRUITS,** **POMELOS, BUDDHA'S** **HANDS)**	● (sliced) ● (supremes) ○ (peel—or Honied Peel on page 36 for the curious)
CITRUS **THIN-SKINNED** **(E.G., CLEMENTINES,** **MANDARINS, MEYER** **LEMONS, KUMQUATS,** **CALAMANSI)**	● (wedges or sliced) ● (whole) ○ (clementine wedges) ● (supremes) ● peeled clementines
COCONUT (FRESH)	● (chunks) ○ (thinly sliced)

CRANBERRIES	● (whole)
CURRANTS	● (whole)
FIGS	● (whole) ● (whole)
GINGER (PREFERABLY YOUNG)	● (chunks) ● (sliced or diced)
GOLDENBERRIES	● (whole)
GOOSEBERRIES	● (whole)
GRAPES	● (in clusters or skewered) ● (whole)
HIBISCUS (FRESH)	● (whole)
KIWIS	● (sliced)
KUMQUATS	● (sliced or quartered) ● (whole) ● (whole)
LYCHEES	● (halved)
MELONS (LESS JUICY MELONS)	● (wedges or sliced) ● (thinly sliced)
MULBERRIES	● (whole)
PAPAYAS	● (wedges or sliced)
PEACHES	● (small halves for any variety or whole for donut variety)
PEARS	● (sliced) ● (whole, small, or peeled) ● (thinly sliced)
PERSIMMONS	● (sliced) ● (thinly sliced)
PINEAPPLES	● (sliced) ● (whole, rounds, small, or peeled) ● (thinly sliced)
PLUMS	● (halved or whole)
PUMPKINS	● (sliced) ● (wedges)
QUINCES	● (sliced) ● (wedges) ● (thinly sliced)
RASPBERRIES	● (whole)
RHUBARB	● (thinly sliced) ● (thinly sliced)
STARFRUITS (CARAMBOLAS)	● (sliced) ● (thinly sliced)
STRAWBERRIES	● (whole) ● (thinly sliced) ● (whole)
TOMATOES (CHERRY OR GRAPE)	● (whole)

Storing, Drying & Finishing

So now that you've candied all this fruit, what next? You've got options. You can store it in syrup, dry it, and then finish it—in that order.

Store it

If I'm not sure how I'm going to use my candied fruit, I store it in its syrup in the refrigerator. This gives me the versatility to just drain it (saving the syrup!—see page 27) and use in recipes as needed, or to dry it for serving in the future.

To store, place the fruit in a clean jar or other airtight container and cover completely with syrup, even if this means filling the jar all the way to the brim with little to no headspace. The more air there is in the jar, the more likely that something like mold will develop (see page 67 for troubleshooting tips). Label and date the jar and store it in the refrigerator, and use a clean utensil when removing any pieces.

Properly candied fruit should keep for at least 4 months this way, and likely longer. If you begin to see mold, cloudiness, or fizziness, check out my troubleshooting section (page 67).

Dry it

Drying is the method I use for serving candied fruit as is, using as décor, using in recipes that can't handle extra humidity, or storing when I have no room left in the refrigerator.

To dry, drain the candied fruit from its syrup (though don't throw that syrup away!—see page 27), then use one of the following methods.

At room temperature: This is the easiest, most hands-off method, the one I usually use despite owning a food dehydrator. That said, it's only a good choice if you live somewhere that isn't super humid. Place fruit on a wire rack set over a rimmed baking sheet. Depending on the temperature and humidity of your home and the moisture content of the fruit, it can take 1 to 3 days to dry this way.

In the oven: This is a good option if you're in a hurry to dry your fruit but don't own a food dehydrator. Preheat the oven to its lowest temperature (likely 150°F to 170°F/65°C to 75°C). Place fruit on a wire rack set over

continued

a rimmed baking sheet. Check the fruit every hour or so—it can take anywhere from 2 to 7 hours depending on the fruit, but you don't want to overdry it.

Using a food dehydrator: This is the best method for drying quickly—it could take anywhere from a couple of hours for fruit chips to overnight for larger pieces. Its low temperature (135°F/57°C) is best for candied fruit and is gentler than the oven, but more powerful than room temperature.

No matter which method you choose, fruit should be dry but still pliable, and if you intend to finish your fruit with a sugar coating, make sure the fruit is still tacky (otherwise the sugar won't stick!).

Once dry, if not serving immediately, store candied fruit in an airtight container. Candied fruit is stable at 75 Brix (that's a measurement for the concentration of sugar; see page 9), but you probably don't have a refractometer (the tool that measures Brix) at home, nor are these methods likely to result in candied fruit that saturated. Still, properly candied and dried fruit should keep at cool room temperature for at least a few months. If you're storing a very humid fruit for a long period, consider keeping it in the refrigerator, just as extra insurance.

Finish it

You can serve candied fruit as is or finish it with a coating of glaze, sugar, or chocolate.

With glaze: A dip in concentrated sugar syrup will create a shiny protective coating. Prepare a syrup by boiling 200 g (1 cup) sugar and 85 mL (⅓ cup) water until the sugar has dissolved. Set a wire rack over a rimmed baking sheet. Use a fork to dip dried candied fruit into the hot syrup, then place on a wire rack to dry overnight.

With sugar: For a sparkly finish, dry the fruit until tacky, then roll it in sugar. You can use granulated, superfine, or flavored sugar (page 62). If the candied fruit is too dry for sugar to stick, dip the fruit briefly in hot water before coating, then let dry completely.

With chocolate: Dip dried candied fruit in tempered chocolate (page 64) and let set before storing somewhere cool and dry.

Finished candy can keep in an airtight container at room temperature for at least a couple of months if properly candied and dried.

Beyond using it in your favorite recipes or the recipes in the next section (page 70) of this book (destined to become your favorites!), you can use candied fruit to decorate cakes and other bakes, garnish cocktails, serve with cheese (trust me), eat on their own, or gift in a candy or chocolate box.

HOW TO

Flavor Sugar Coatings

If you're going to finish your candied fruit with sugar, flavoring the coating sugar is a very good idea. The simplest, best addition you can make is citric acid—a technique I learned from Nashville pastry chef Rebekah Turshen. When fruit is cooked (and especially candied), it loses its acidity; you can restore that fresh taste with 1 tablespoon citric acid per 200 g (1 cup) sugar, or you can double it for a sour-candy effect.

Other dried flavorings, such as ground spices, coffee, chilis, or salt, are easy embellishments. If you want to flavor the sugar with something that contains water, such as alcohol or fresh herbs, you'll just need to dry it out after mixing in the flavoring. Add enough liquid to make the sugar resemble wet sand, or pulse sugar with herbs in a food processor until it has the same texture. Spread the mixture in a thin layer and dry in a food dehydrator at 135°F (57°C), or spread it on a rimmed baking sheet and dry in the oven at its lowest temperature. It should take a few hours to dry either way. Remove from the dehydrator or oven and cool, then grind it in a food processor or spice grinder before using.

Vanilla sugar is nice as well and is a good way to use spent pods. I keep a perpetual jar of it on my counter, filling it back up with sugar whenever it's getting low. Every time I scrape the seeds from a vanilla pod, I throw the pod in the jar, which perfumes the sugar in a heavenly fashion. If I've fished the pod out of a jam or custard, I just rinse it off, let it dry, then toss it in.

Salt, Aleppo pepper,
and citric acid sugar
coating

Basil sugar coating

Campari
sugar coating

HOW TO

Temper Chocolate

To coat candied fruits in shiny, snappy chocolate that is stable at room temperature, you'll need to temper the chocolate, which is different from simply melting chocolate. If you straight-up melt chocolate and use it to dip fruit, the chocolate will probably take on a white bloom or dusty coating within a few hours and look like an old chocolate bar you bought from a gas station in a ghost town.

Tempering can be intimidating, but it's actually not that hard. I've successfully tempered chocolate while crying during an argument (which I don't recommend, but it did still work)! It does take practice and a good instant-read thermometer, however.

Make sure any fruit you're coating in chocolate is dry (it can be tacky but not moist) and at room temperature.

MICROWAVE METHOD: Now that I own a microwave, this is the method I'm most likely to use because it's so dang easy. Start with either chocolate callets or chopped couverture. Weigh it in a heatproof bowl, then remove 25% and set aside.

Microwave on medium heat for 45 seconds, then stir. Continue heating on medium in 15-second intervals, stirring each time, until almost completely melted. The temperature of the chocolate must not exceed 105°F (40°C).

A little at a time, add the remaining chocolate, stirring until melted before adding more.

Keep stirring until the temperature of the chocolate has dropped to 89°F to 90°F (31°C to 32°C) for dark chocolate or 85°F to 87°F (29°C to 30°C) for milk or white chocolate. Test the temper by taking a little piece of parchment and dipping it in the chocolate. Wait a few minutes to see if it sets and is shiny. If yes, use immediately. If not, start over. If it cools down too much, microwave it for 10 seconds at a time on medium.

STOVETOP METHOD: This is pretty much the same as the microwave method but uses a double boiler. Place 75% of the chocolate in a heatproof bowl set over a pot of simmering water. Stir until just melted, never letting the temperature exceed 105°F (40°C) (you may have to move the bowl on and off the pot).

Remove the bowl from the pot and, a little at a time, add the remaining 25% chocolate, stirring until melted before adding more.

Keep stirring until the temperature of the chocolate has dropped to 89°F to 90°F (31°C to 32°C) for dark chocolate or 85°F to 87°F (29°C to 30°C) for milk or white chocolate. Test the temper by taking a little piece of parchment paper and dipping it in the chocolate. Wait a few minutes to see if it sets and is shiny. If yes, use immediately. If not, start over. If it cools down too much, briefly stir over a pot of simmering water.

If you have any chocolate left over, just spread it on parchment paper. Let it harden, then chop it up and add it to your next batch of chocolate chip cookies.

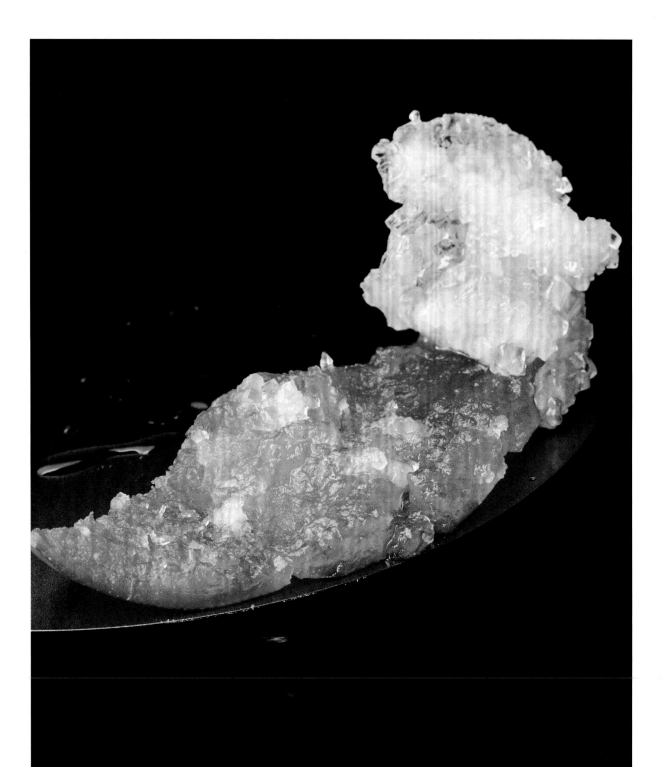

Troubleshooting

While my sincere wish is that all your candying goes off without a hitch, sometimes things will go wrong in spite of your best intentions. Hopefully this section will address some of the troubles you're most likely to run up against, so you can either fix them or learn for next time.

Cooking problems

Caramelization: If your fruit has caramelized, with the syrup going from clear to amber (or darker), you've overcooked it. Next time, make sure you keep an eye on the pot, especially toward the end of cooking. All is not lost, however, if it's not too far gone. As long as it tastes good, keep it, but the syrup might be so thick that you'll have to rinse it off!

Disintegrating fruit: If your fruit falls apart during candying, it either started out overripe or too soft, or it got overcooked during simmering or blanching. Always start with very fresh, preferably slightly underripe, fruit. If precooking, make sure to do so just enough to tenderize the fruit without it getting too soft or breaking down.

Tough skin or peel: The most likely culprit here is inadequate blanching. Make sure that any thick citrus peel going into syrup has been cooked enough that there is no visible white pith. Additionally, make sure to start with fresh fruit—older citrus fruit can be dry and tough. Another possibility is that the sugar density of the syrup increased too quickly. Next time try the Whole-ish method (page 28), which increases the sugar density gradually.

Storage problems

Crystallization: First off, see How to Prevent Crystallization (page 11). You need to add an invert sugar or acid to make sure the sucrose in solution doesn't crystallize— maybe you didn't add enough? To fix crystallized fruit, rinse under hot water in a sieve to remove any large crystals, then cover with fresh hot simple syrup to which you've added 1 tablespoon light corn syrup for each 250 g (1 cup) water. Or, if the crystallization is not too dramatic (not covered in an impenetrable layer of huge sugar crystals) and you want to use it right away, simply rinse the fruit under hot water to wash away large crystals, or simply cut them off before using. I've done this, I assure you! The candied fruit can then be dried as instructed on page 59.

continued

Fermentation: After a while, your candied fruit in syrup may begin to ferment, especially if the syrup is not highly concentrated or if the storage conditions are subpar. The telltale signs are a bulging lid, a hissing sound when you open the jar, bubbles, and a sour taste. Next time, use the fruit sooner and make sure it's stored in an adequately cold refrigerator in a clean jar with little to no headspace. That said, before you dispose of fermented fruit, taste it! I once lost a jar of candied cranberries, which have a relatively low sugar concentration, in the back of the refrigerator for months. When I finally unearthed it, it was fermented—but also delicious! I drained the syrup and used it to flavor sparkling water, and I dried the cranberries and made the best craisins I'd ever tasted. A happy accident indeed.

Mold: Mold can potentially develop on candied fruit stored in syrup in the refrigerator or dried and stored at room temperature. When fruit in syrup develops mold, it might be because the refrigerator wasn't sufficiently cold, there was too much headspace (and thus air) in the storage container, or the syrup wasn't sufficiently concentrated in the first place. If mold does develop, it probably won't do so for at least a few months, so one solution is to use your fruit in syrup within a few months. If mold has developed, however, I usually choose to save fruit that's particularly precious to me, especially if it's just a little mold. Scoop off the visible mold, drain and rinse the fruit in hot water, then dry (page 59) and use within a month.

If mold develops on dried candied fruit, throw it out. This probably happened because it was either insufficiently candied, insufficiently dried, or stored somewhere too hot and/or humid. Store plump dried candied fruit in the refrigerator (if you have space) and use it within a few months.

Stickiness: If your dried candied fruit is getting all sticky, you're either storing it somewhere too humid or you didn't dry it enough. Little silica packs can help prevent this problem if you're unable to control the humidity otherwise. You can also try finishing with glaze (page 60), which acts as a protective coating and reduces potential stickiness.

BA

PART II

KELTIE

Baking Notes

If you haven't already gobbled up all your candied fruit or given it away in vegan bonbon boxes, it's time to get baking. The recipes that follow are variously beloved classics, bakes inspired by beloved classics, or newfangled ways to get more candied fruit into your homemade desserts.

Unfortunately, there's no possible way I can cover the vast array of ways people use candied fruit all over the globe, nor did I want to create recipes for dishes I've never tried before. Instead, I hope the techniques in the previous section can help you master candied fruit and thus make your rosca de reyes or ba bao fan or cannoli even better than it already is. But if you're looking for a recipe for Mendiants (page 139), Old-Fashioned Carrot Pudding (page 156), or Nesselrode Pie (page 151), I've got you covered.

Always read a recipe all the way through so you can prepare. That way there are no surprises. If you're in a pinch and realize you can't candy the fruit you need or fear you won't have enough time, don't fret! Check out the simplifications for ways to use canned or store-bought fruit (page 13) instead. The recipes will still turn out delicious. I've also included some creative substitution ideas I've tried if you want to mix it up.

But first, let's talk ingredients. For best results, you ideally want to use the same—or as close as possible to the same—ingredients as I did when developing these recipes. So unless otherwise indicated:

- *Butter:* Unsalted

- *Chocolate:* Best quality you can afford, preferably in the form of callets/pistoles/feves

- *Cocoa:* Best quality you can afford, preferably extra-dark alkalized (Dutch process)

- *Eggs:* Large, free-range if possible

- *Gelatin:* Sheets, but if you can't find them, use powdered. One envelope of powdered gelatin (7 g/2½ teaspoons) equals five sheets

- *Neutral oil:* Grapeseed preferably, but use whatever you've got

- *Olive oil:* Extra-virgin

continued

- *Salt:* Diamond Crystal kosher; if using Morton, use three-quarters of the amount in the recipe, and if using table salt, use half the amount

- *Sugar:* Granulated

In terms of tools and equipment, hopefully your kitchen has standard baking tools like a wire cooling rack, baking sheets, parchment paper (or silicone mats), and pastry brushes. If not, that's okay, but I encourage you to procure these items because most cookbooks call for them. Here are a few other tools, pieces of equipment, and notes to consider as you bake your way through these recipes:

- *Baking pans:* A good starter set of pans includes a straight-sided 8-inch square, a 9 × 13-inch rectangular, a 9-inch springform, a 9-inch tart with removable bottom, and a 10- to 12-cup Bundt. You'll also notice I use two 7-inch round pans for my layer cakes (page 96). Beyond those, in this book you'll find me using a popover pan, a madeleine pan, a pudding basin, and ramekins. These are fun to have but can almost always be substituted with more common items such as muffin tins, stainless-steel bowls, and wide-mouth jars.

- *Decorative molds:* Unsurprisingly, ornate molds for old-fashioned desserts like jellies are easiest to find in thrift stores or on eBay. They come in all shapes and sizes and look beautiful hung on the wall when not in use. But if you aren't a collector, you can use anything else with the same capacity. The clean lines of a stainless-steel bowl will look modern and sleek!

- *Ice cream scoops:* I prefer to portion cookie dough using an ice cream scoop, as it's easy and consistent and makes good-looking cookies. That said, you can also portion with tablespoons or a scale (divide the weight of the dough by the yield) and roll by hand.

- *Scale:* I will never stop singing the praises of baking by weight using a scale. It's far more precise, results in a better finished product, and creates way less dishes!

- *Stand mixer:* If you bake a lot, this is an indispensable piece of gear, but mixers can also be prohibitively expensive. Fortunately, you can make any of these recipes with electric beaters or elbow grease instead. I often don't bother getting my mixer out if I'm just whipping or creaming a small quantity of something.

CAKES

of all

PERSUASIONS

Red Currant Cupcakes

I know fancy layer cakes are all the rage right now, but personally I've never turned my back on the cupcake. I especially love their portability in summer. I brought these to a picnic for my mother-in-law's 70th birthday, and she wouldn't stop raving about how the currants looked "frozen"! Their sharp acidity really makes these little cakes pop, and their juice tints the buttercream a romantic pink.

You'll need to make currant juice for the frosting, but it's a doddle. Make a lot and do jelly at the same time! Or make the small amount, and if you have any left over, use it for a spritzer, sweetening to taste.

Makes 12 cupcakes

For the Cupcakes

187 g (1⅓ cups) all-purpose flour

1¼ tsp baking powder

¼ tsp salt

115 g (½ cup) unsalted butter, at room temperature

200 g (1 cup) sugar

2 eggs

½ tsp vanilla extract

125 mL (½ cup) whole milk

125 g (¾ cup) stemmed red currants

For the Red Currant Buttercream

125 g (¾ cup) red currants

1 recipe Custard Buttercream (page 195)

Preheat the oven to 350°F (175°C). Line a 12-cup muffin tin with paper liners.

To make the cupcakes, in a small bowl, whisk the flour, baking powder, and salt.

In the bowl of a stand mixer fitted with the paddle attachment, beat the butter and sugar until light and fluffy. Add the eggs one at a time, beating well after each addition. Add the vanilla.

With the mixer running on low speed, add one-third of the flour mixture and then half the milk. Repeat until everything is incorporated. Fold in the currants. Divide the batter evenly among the muffin cups.

Bake until a toothpick inserted in the center comes out clean, about 25 minutes. Cool completely on a wire rack.

continued

To Finish

6 stems red currants,
  crystallized (page 49)

6 stems white currants,
  crystallized (page 49)

———————

SIMPLIFY *Frozen currants also work well in the cake batter and to make the juice. If you don't have it in you to make red currant juice, use store-bought or simply omit, tinting the buttercream with food coloring if you like.*

SUBSTITUTE *No red or white currants? Use any tart berry—black currants, sour cherries, gooseberries, raspberries . . .*

NOTE *A jelly bag can be many things, as long as it's clean! I use a nut milk bag, but you can also use a double layer of cheesecloth, an old T-shirt or pantyhose, a paint strainer . . . or an actual jelly bag. A fine-mesh sieve could even do the trick in this instance.*

———————

To make the red currant buttercream, in a pot, cover the currants with water and bring to a boil. Reduce the heat and gently simmer for about 30 minutes, until they look pale and deflated—exhausted, really. Strain the mixture through a jelly bag (see Note) and squeeze out all you can into a clean vessel (I like to let it drip overnight as if I'm making jelly, but it's not necessary here). Beat 60 mL (¼ cup) red currant juice into the buttercream until well combined.

To finish, frost the cupcakes with buttercream and garnish with a crystallized currant stem. The cupcakes will keep at room temperature overnight or for up to 3 days in an airtight container in the fridge. Just bring them to room temperature before serving.

Syrup-Soaked Citrus Olive Oil Cornmeal Cake

This cornmeal cake looks deceptively plain but is a textural joy and flavor punch thanks to a soaking with what I unofficially call a sweet vinaigrette—candied orange syrup, olive oil, lemon juice, and salt. I developed it when I worked at a wonderful bakery in Toronto called Robinson Bread, where we changed the flavor of our pound cake seasonally. At the time, we were coming off Christmas and had loads of leftover syrup from candying orange peel to work with. I was also obsessed with a syrup- and amaro-soaked cake that Michelle Marek (page 93) had made. Meanwhile, I was toying with a syrup-based salad dressing concept (which is still not there). Combining these inspirations and many cornmeal cake tests later, I feel I've landed on the perfect midmorning or afternoon snack. It would also be welcome as a dessert paired with fruit compote and cream, or even just alongside a glass of wine.

Makes one 5 × 9-inch loaf cake

For the Cake

375 g (1¾ cups + 2 Tbsp) sugar

Zest of 1 orange

275 g (1 cup + 3 Tbsp) unsalted butter, at room temperature

60 mL (¼ cup) extra-virgin olive oil

5 eggs, at room temperature

245 g (1¾ cups) all-purpose flour

100 g (½ cup + 1 Tbsp) coarse-ground cornmeal

1¼ tsp baking powder

½ tsp salt

Preheat the oven to 350°F (175°C). Grease a 5 × 9-inch loaf pan and line with parchment paper.

To make the cake, in the bowl of a stand mixer, combine the sugar and orange zest and rub together with your fingertips to perfume the sugar. Add the butter and oil, and cream with the paddle attachment on medium speed until light and fluffy. Add the eggs one at a time, beating well after each addition and scraping down the bowl if necessary. Add the flour, cornmeal, baking powder, and salt and mix on low until incorporated. Scrape down the sides of the bowl, then whip on medium speed for 10 seconds.

continued

For the Soak

125 mL (½ cup) candied
    orange syrup (pages 56–57)

2 Tbsp lemon juice

2 Tbsp extra-virgin olive oil

Pinch of salt

Transfer the batter to the prepared pan, smoothing the top with a small offset spatula. Bake for 1 hour and 5 minutes to 1 hour and 15 minutes, until a toothpick inserted in the center comes out clean. Meanwhile, make the soak.

To make the soak, in a small bowl or measuring cup, whisk the syrup, lemon juice, oil, and salt.

As soon as the cake comes out of the oven, transfer the pan to a wire rack. Use a pastry brush to brush the soak onto the surface of the cake until it has all been absorbed. Let cool completely before unmolding the cake.

The cake will keep, well wrapped, at room temperature for up to 7 days.

SUBSTITUTE *No candied orange syrup? Use any candied citrus syrup (pages 56–57).*

Quince & Mascarpone Cheesecake

Of course, I don't like to pick favorites . . . but this might be my favorite recipe in the book. Not only is it positively stunning, with its quince chips encased in sunset-pink translucent jelly as if in amber, but I could eat the whole thing myself. Thick, snappy, and buttery wholemeal base? Check. Airy, rich, and tangy no-bake mascarpone cheesecake? Check. Fragrant and sweet-tart topping? As mentioned, check. Perfection (if I do say so myself).

Serves 12

For the Crust

230 g (2 cups) digestive biscuit crumbs

115 g (½ cup) unsalted butter, melted

½ tsp salt

For the Cheesecake

500 g (two 8 oz packages) brick-style cream cheese, at room temperature

250 g (1 cup) mascarpone

1 (398 mL/14 oz) can sweetened condensed milk

2 g (1 sheet) gelatin, soaked (optional)

60 mL (¼ cup) lemon juice

1 tsp vanilla extract

¼ tsp salt

Grease a 9-inch springform pan.

To make the crust, in a medium bowl, combine the biscuit crumbs, melted butter, and salt. Press firmly into the bottom of the prepared pan. Chill in the refrigerator until firm, 1 to 2 hours.

To make the cheesecake, in the bowl of a stand mixer fitted with the paddle attachment, beat the cream cheese and mascarpone until smooth. Gradually add the sweetened condensed milk.

If using the gelatin, warm the lemon juice in the microwave or in a small pot over medium heat. Dissolve the gelatin in the lemon juice, then beat into the bowl of the stand mixer. Otherwise, beat in the cool lemon juice.

Add the vanilla and salt and mix. Pour onto the prepared crust, smoothing the top with a small offset spatula. Chill in the refrigerator until firm, 2 to 3 hours.

continued

To Finish

310 g (1 cup) quince jelly

2 g (1 sheet) gelatin, soaked (optional)

1 recipe candied quince chips (page 40), preferably in syrup, drained

To finish, melt the quince jelly gently in a small pot over medium-low heat or in a heatproof bowl in the microwave in 30-second increments. Stir in the gelatin, if using. Let cool until no longer hot but still pourable. Meanwhile, arrange the candied quince chips in a decorative pattern on top of the cheesecake—you will have extra chips, which can be stored (page 40) for later. Pour the melted jelly evenly over top to cover. Chill in the refrigerator until set, about 1 hour.

Unmold the cake and serve cold, using a hot, dry knife to cut clean slices.

The cake will keep, covered, in the refrigerator for up to 3 days.

SIMPLIFY *The cheesecake is still amazing on its own without the quince topping. Serve topped with compote, jam, or fresh fruit.*

SUBSTITUTE *No digestives? Use graham or arrowroot crumbs. No quince jelly? Use crabapple or another tart red- or orange-hued jelly. No mascarpone? Use labneh, which will make the cake a little tarter and a little less rich. No quince? You can make one recipe of candied apple chips (page 40) or encase fresh currants in currant jelly.*

Tropical Terrazzo Cake

"They paused to breathe in steam rising from the oven and took extra helpings of pound cake sliced to reveal a terrazzo pattern of candied citron and glace fruits," writes John Birdsall in one of my favorite culinary biographies, *The Man Who Ate Too Much*. The idea for this sturdy pound cake studded with chunks of candied tropical fruits and glazed with tart lime syrup came from that single line in this biography of icon James Beard. The book is full of literary descriptions like this that pull you right into the action, making it a pleasure to read. Most importantly, the book doesn't downplay his queerness. I recommend reading it while you enjoy a slice of this cake. Use a variety of candied tropical (or tropical-adjacent) fruits, keeping in mind that it can always be a mixture of homemade and store-bought. I usually use pineapple, kiwi, papaya, citron, ginger, and cactus pear.

Serves 16

For the Cake

230 g (1 cup) unsalted butter, at room temperature (very soft)

533 g (2⅔ cups) sugar

1½ tsp salt

Zest of 1 lime

6 eggs, at room temperature

420 g (3 cups) all-purpose flour

250 mL (1 cup) full-fat coconut milk

500 g (2 cups) drained and chopped (½- to 1-inch pieces) mixed candied fruit (pages 56–57), reserving the syrup

Preheat the oven to 350°F (175°C). Generously grease and amply flour a 10- to 12-cup Bundt pan and refrigerate the pan until it's time to fill it.

To make the cake, in the bowl of a stand mixer fitted with the paddle attachment, cream the butter, sugar, salt, and lime zest until light and fluffy. Add the eggs one at a time, beating well after each addition.

With the mixer running on low speed, add one-third of the flour and then half of the coconut milk. Alternate until all the flour and coconut milk are incorporated. Scrape down the sides of the bowl, then beat on medium-high for 30 seconds to make sure everything is well blended. Fold in the chopped candied fruit.

Transfer the batter to the prepared pan. Give the pan a hard tap on the countertop to help settle the batter. Bake for 1 hour and 10 minutes to 1 hour and 20 minutes, or until a toothpick inserted in the center comes out clean.

Cool on a wire rack for 10 minutes. Meanwhile, make the syrup.

continued

For the Syrup

125 mL (½ cup) candied fruit
    syrup (see Note)

60 mL (¼ cup) lime juice

2 Tbsp dark rum (optional)

To make the syrup, in a small pot, combine the syrup and lime juice. Bring to a boil and cook until it is reduced by half. Remove from the heat and stir in the rum, if using.

To assemble, carefully turn the cake out of the pan. Use all the syrup to brush the cake all over the top and sides. Cool completely.

The cake will keep, well wrapped, at room temperature for at least 5 days.

NOTE *You can use any candied fruit syrup (pages 56–57) for this recipe or use the reserved syrup from the cake method.*

DELIGHTS AND PREJUDICES

Stollen Pound Cake

I love stollen, the rich German Christmas bread full of candied fruit, especially the version with a thick vein of marzipan running through the center. But I'll be honest with you—when I'm feeling lazy, I'm not always up for a yeasted dough, what with its kneading and rising and shaping. Thus, I created this very easy-to-make pound cake, with all the flavors of stollen (except for yeasty) and complete with a marzipan tunnel, and it's pretty impressive in its own right! This is particularly true if you bring it to the table on a beautiful cake stand garnished with candied cranberries and crystallized rosemary. As far as mixed fruit goes, use whatever you like, but I usually go for some mix of citrus, cherries, and quince. Note: You will want to start this the night before.

Serves 16

---

185 g (¾ cup) mixed diced candied fruits (pages 56–57)

120 g (¾ cup) golden raisins

60 g (½ cup) slivered almonds

125 mL (½ cup) dark rum

420 g (3 cups) all-purpose flour

2 tsp Mixed Spice (page 196)

1 tsp baking powder

1 tsp salt

½ tsp baking soda

300 g (1½ cups) sugar

Zest of 1 orange

Zest of 1 lemon

230 g (1 cup) unsalted butter, at room temperature

4 eggs, at room temperature

The night before you make the cake, in a medium bowl, combine the candied fruits, raisins, almonds, and rum. Cover and let sit overnight at room temperature.

The next day, preheat the oven to 350°F (175°C). Grease a 12-cup Bundt or tube pan well with butter and dust with flour.

In a small bowl, whisk the flour, mixed spice, baking powder, salt, and baking soda.

In the bowl of a stand mixer, place the sugar and use your fingertips to rub in the orange and lemon zest. Add the room-temperature butter and fit the mixer with the paddle attachment. Cream on medium speed until light and fluffy, 3 to 5 minutes. Add the eggs one at a time, beating well after each addition, followed by the almond extract.

continued

1 tsp almond extract

250 g (1 cup) sour cream

230 g (8 oz) marzipan

77 g (⅓ cup) unsalted butter, melted

63–125 g (½–1 cup) icing sugar, for dusting

Optional Garnishes

Candied cranberries (page 39)

Crystallized fresh bay leaves (page 49)

Crystallized rosemary (page 49)

With the mixer running on low speed, add one-third of the flour mixture and then half of the sour cream. Alternate until all the flour and sour cream are incorporated. Add the candied fruit mixture (including any liquid at the bottom of the bowl) and mix until incorporated.

Transfer half of the batter to the prepared pan. Roll the marzipan into an even rope and form it into a circle that will fit in the center. Place the marzipan circle in the center of the batter and cover with the remaining batter.

Bake for 1 hour to 1 hour and 15 minutes, or until a toothpick inserted in the center comes out clean. Cool on a wire rack for 15 minutes before unmolding.

Using a pastry brush, paint the top and sides of the cake with the melted butter, then sift half of the icing sugar over top. There's no easy way to get full coverage, as with a traditional stollen—you have to use your hands to pat the icing sugar on the sides. Keep patting until the icing sugar sticks and is dusted to your liking, so use as much as you need, but reserve some for sifting. Let cool completely, then sift the remaining icing sugar over top. Decorate with candied cranberries, crystallized bay leaves, or crystallized rosemary, if desired.

The cake will keep, covered, at room temperature for at least 5 days.

Apricot & Orange Roll Cake

Michelle Marek is many things—pastry chef, chef chef, food stylist (of this very book!), ceramicist, cat lover, Vermonter, and a very dear old friend. Case in point, she made me this ethereal cake for my 41st birthday (all the more special since pastry people are very rarely made birthday cakes). The orange and olive oil sponge (substantial yet somehow light) is rolled up around a rich, whipped mascarpone (which is also used to ice it) and apricot jam enhanced with candied peel. Best of all, it's finished with the sweetest little candied peel flowers to dress it up for a special occasion.

Serves 8 to 10

For the Cake

83 g (½ cup + 1½ Tbsp) all-purpose flour

113 g (¼ cup + 3 Tbsp) sugar, divided, plus more for dusting

¾ tsp baking powder

¼ tsp salt

2 egg yolks

45 mL (3 Tbsp) extra-virgin olive oil

Zest of ½ orange

45 mL (3 Tbsp) orange juice

½ tsp vanilla extract

4 egg whites

¼ tsp cream of tartar

Preheat the oven to 350°F (175°C). Grease a quarter sheet pan and line with parchment paper.

To make the cake, in a small bowl, whisk the flour, 75 g (¼ cup + 2 tablespoons) sugar, baking powder, and salt. In a medium bowl, whisk the yolks, olive oil, orange zest and juice, and vanilla. Whisk in the dry ingredients to combine.

In the bowl of a stand mixer fitted with the whisk attachment, whisk the egg whites with the cream of tartar on medium speed until frothy. Increase the speed to medium-high and whisk until soft peaks begin to form. Gradually add the remaining sugar and beat until stiff and glossy. Fold one-third of the meringue into the cake mixture to lighten, then fold in the remaining meringue just until incorporated.

continued

For the Filling

150 g (½ cup) apricot jam

2 Tbsp diced candied orange
    peel (page 33)

250 mL (1 cup) whipping cream

34 g (¼ cup + 1 tsp) icing sugar

175 g (¾ cup) mascarpone

To Finish

Small handful candied orange
    peels (page 33), shaped into
    flowers (page 54)

SIMPLIFY *No candied peel?*
Simply omit!

SUBSTITUTE *No candied orange*
peel flowers? Use dried apricot fruits
déguisés (page 47) or crystallized
violets (page 49). Change up the fruit
filling and garnish as you see fit.

Transfer the batter to the prepared pan, smoothing out the top with a small offset spatula. Bake for 18 to 22 minutes, until the cake is golden brown and springs back when touched. Let cool on a wire rack for 5 minutes.

Dust a clean, damp tea towel generously with sugar, then invert the cake onto it while still warm. Roll up the cake and sugared tea towel together toward the long side of the cake. Let cool completely at room temperature.

To make the filling, in a small bowl, stir together the jam and candied peel. In the bowl of a stand mixer fitted with the whisk attachment, whip the cream with the icing sugar until medium peaks form. Add the mascarpone and whip until stiff peaks form.

Unroll the cake, then spread the jam mixture evenly over top, leaving a ½-inch border on one long side. Cover the jam with half of the mascarpone mixture. Starting at the long side without a border, carefully roll up the cake while at the same time peeling off the tea towel clinging to it. Transfer to a platter seam side down and refrigerate to firm up a bit, around 15 minutes.

To finish, use a serrated knife to trim about ½ inch off each end to clean the ends. Use the remaining mascarpone cream to ice the roll, then decorate with the candied orange flowers. Chill for at least 1 hour before serving or up to overnight.

Ideally, serve after chilling. It will still keep up to 4 days but will not be as presentable.

HOW TO

Make a Layer Cake My Way

Although I've always loved a layer cake, I really refined my personal technique and style in the great pandemic-induced Internet fancy-cake revival. I teach a whole workshop about it, but there are a few hot tips that you should know if you want to make either of the layer cake recipes that follow.

- Personally, I think an 8-inch layer cake is too big for most scenarios I find myself in. It can easily feed 20, especially after a big celebratory meal. I prefer to make 7-inch cakes, which can handily feed 12. This size of lightweight metal pan is affordable and easy to procure. You'll need two, and you will have to get comfy slicing the cakes in half horizontally to make four layers. If you simply must make a bigger cake, you can double these recipes for 8-inch pans.

- To make slicing easier, it's best to bake the cakes at least one day in advance so that, once cooled, you can wrap and refrigerate them overnight before frosting. This will make them much easier to handle.

- If you're relatively new to making layer cakes, it can be helpful to make extra buttercream to have on hand just in case. If you have any left over, you can either freeze it to use as backup next time or use it in the next few days to make something else. Custard buttercream is a great filling for Victoria sponge, sandwich cookies, or macarons.

- Layer cakes are really best enjoyed at room temperature, so if you're planning to serve yours the day you make it, there's no need to refrigerate unless it's very hot or you're planning on transporting it.

- Most importantly, have fun! Like any skill, building and frosting a layer cake perfectly takes a lot of practice, but it's a delicious journey. Be creative with what you've got.

Pear, Hazelnut & Caramel Layer Cake

This sleek caramel-colored cake sports a dramatic crown of translucent pear chips and a single caramelized hazelnut in the middle. Swaths of salted caramel buttercream cloak a moist and nutty hazelnut and rye flour cake, with chunks of caramel-steeped pears nestled between the layers—except for the one layer filled only with roasted hazelnut–studded caramel. Need I say more?

One note, though: If it's a particularly humid day, the pear chips might start to droop. This happened when I first created the cake for my spouse's birthday. You can either apply them at the last minute or do what I did: fold them down over the top of the cake, which creates an equally beautiful decoration. Find more layer cake–specific tips on the opposite page.

Makes one 4-layer, 7-inch cake

For the Cakes

105 g (¾ cup) all-purpose flour

60 g (½ cup) hazelnut meal

50 g (6 Tbsp) rye flour

¾ tsp baking powder

¾ tsp salt

¼ tsp baking soda

125 mL (½ cup) whole milk

125 mL (½ cup) neutral oil

½ tsp vanilla extract

2 eggs

175 g (¾ cup + 2 Tbsp) sugar

Preheat the oven to 350°F (175°C). Grease two 7-inch round pans and line the bottoms with parchment paper.

To make the cakes, in a small bowl, whisk the all-purpose flour, hazelnut meal, rye flour, baking powder, salt, and baking soda. In a measuring cup, combine the milk, oil, and vanilla.

In the bowl of a stand mixer fitted with the whisk attachment, whisk the eggs and sugar on medium-high speed until the mixture is pale, thick, and doubled in volume. With the mixer running on low speed, add one-third of the flour mixture and one-third of the milk mixture. Repeat until all of each mixture has been mixed in. Divide the batter equally between the pans and bake until a toothpick inserted in the center comes out clean, 30 to 35 minutes.

Let the pans cool on a wire rack for 10 minutes, then unmold the cakes and allow to cool completely. The cakes will keep, wrapped in plastic wrap, in the refrigerator for up to 3 days or in the freezer for up to 3 months.

continued

For Assembly

380 g (1½ cups) Caramel
  (page 193)

1 recipe Custard Buttercream
  (page 195)

125 g (½ cup + ⅓ cup) toasted
  skinned hazelnuts, divided

4 quarters Caramel Pears
  (page 180), sliced ¼ inch thick

125 mL (½ cup) Caramel Pears
  syrup (page 180)

1 recipe candied pear chips
  (page 40)

1 candied caramelized hazelnut
  (page 47) (optional)

To assemble, in the bowl of a stand mixer fitted with the whisk attachment, whip half of the caramel into the buttercream until fully incorporated. Finely chop 75 g (½ cup) hazelnuts and fold into the remaining caramel.

Using a serrated knife, cut both cakes in half horizontally. Use a dab of buttercream to affix the bottom of one cake to a cake board or serving platter. Brush a little caramel syrup all over the cake to moisten. Use an offset spatula to spread a ½-inch layer of buttercream over the cake. Top with half of the pears.

Place the other half of the cake, cut side up, on top of the first layer. Brush with syrup, then pipe a buttercream border around the edge using a ½-inch plain tip. Fill the center with the caramel-hazelnut mixture.

Place the top of the second cake, cut side up, on the previous layer. Brush with syrup, then spread with a ½-inch layer of buttercream and top with the remaining pears. Place the final cake layer, cut side down, on top and brush with syrup.

Using a palette knife, coat the cake with a thin layer of buttercream. Chill in the refrigerator for 10 to 15 minutes to firm up. Frost the cake with the remaining buttercream and finish with a ring of remaining hazelnuts around the bottom. Make a slightly overlapping ring of pear chips around the top of the cake, affixing the bottom third of the pears to the buttercream. Finally, place a single hazelnut, caramelized or otherwise, in the center of the cake.

The finished cake will keep, covered, at cool room temperature overnight or in the refrigerator for up to 5 days. Bring to room temperature before serving.

SIMPLIFY *Use store-bought canned pears or even buttery ripe fresh pears. Use store-bought dulce de leche instead of making caramel.*

Quince, Chestnut & Chocolate Layer Cake

If you want to know how special I think this cake is, suffice to say it was my wedding cake (albeit a little larger and two-tiered). Some of the ingredients can be hard to track down, depending on where you live, but they're all worth procuring. It calls for chestnut flour, a deliciously earthy gluten-free flour. Chestnut cream, another worthy ingredient, makes delightful desserts—the truffles on page 143, for instance. This cake is truly fit for any celebration—just check out my tips on page 96 to make baking this a piece of cake.

Makes one 4-layer, 7-inch cake

For the Cakes

140 g (1 cup) all-purpose flour

70 g (½ cup) chestnut flour

¾ tsp baking powder

¾ tsp salt

¼ tsp baking soda

125 mL (½ cup) whole milk

125 mL (½ cup) neutral oil

½ tsp vanilla extract

2 eggs

175 g (¾ cup + 2 Tbsp) sugar

15 g (½ oz) finely grated dark chocolate

Preheat the oven to 350°F (175°C). Grease two 7-inch round pans and line the bottoms with parchment paper.

To make the cakes, in a small bowl, whisk the all-purpose and chestnut flours, baking powder, salt, and baking soda. In a measuring cup, combine the milk, oil, and vanilla.

In the bowl of a stand mixer fitted with the whisk attachment, whisk the eggs and sugar on medium-high speed until the mixture is pale, thick, and doubled in volume. With the mixer running on low speed, add one-third of the flour mixture and one-third of the milk mixture. Repeat until all of each mixture has been mixed in. Fold in the grated chocolate. Divide the batter equally between the pans and bake until a toothpick inserted in the center comes out clean, 30 to 35 minutes.

Let the pans cool on a wire rack for 10 minutes, then unmold the cakes and allow to cool completely. The cakes will keep, wrapped in plastic wrap, in the refrigerator for up to 3 days or in the freezer for up to 3 months.

continued

For Assembly

1 recipe Custard Buttercream (page 195)

75 g (¼ cup) chestnut cream

60 g (2 oz) dark chocolate, melted

1 candied quince (page 25), in syrup (you will need 60 mL/¼ cup syrup)

60 mL (¼ cup) cognac

1 recipe candied quince chips (page 40)

1 candied chestnut (page 28 or 33)

Gold leaf (optional)

SIMPLIFY *Use poached quince or store-bought canned quince (try an Eastern European grocer!) instead of candied. Alternatively, use crumbled candied chestnuts. No cognac? Use all quince syrup.*

To assemble, in the bowl of a stand mixer fitted with the whisk attachment, whip half of the buttercream with the chestnut cream and chocolate until fully incorporated. In a small bowl, combine 60 mL (¼ cup) candied quince syrup with the cognac.

Using a serrated knife, cut both cakes in half horizontally. Use a dab of buttercream to affix the bottom of one cake to a cake board or serving platter. Brush the cognac-quince syrup all over the cake to moisten. Using a plain ½-inch tip, pipe a border of plain buttercream around the edges of the cake. Use an offset spatula to fill the center in with chestnut-chocolate buttercream. Top with one-third of the candied quince.

Repeat twice more, placing the cake cut side up on the previous layer. Brush with more syrup, then, using a palette knife, coat the cake with a thin layer of buttercream. Place the second bottom half, cut side down, on top of the cake as the final layer. Brush with syrup, then, using a palette knife, coat the cake with a thin layer of plain buttercream.

Chill in the refrigerator for 10 to 15 minutes to firm up. Frost the cake with the remaining plain buttercream, reserving about 125 mL (½ cup) for piping the borders. Decorate the sides and top of the cake with quince chips in an artful pattern. Using a medium star tip, pipe a border around the bottom and then the top of the cake. Finally, pipe a rosette in the center of the cake and place the candied chestnut on top. Decorate with a gold leaf, if desired.

The finished cake will keep, covered, at cool room temperature overnight or in the refrigerator for up to 5 days. Bring to room temperature before serving.

44 Cordial Babas

44 cordial is a liqueur made by filling slits in an orange with 44 coffee beans and then steeping it for 44 days in rum with 44 teaspoons sugar. This isn't exactly that—it won't take 44 days!—but those flavors are the inspiration for these babas, one of my very favorite desserts. Rich yeasted dough is studded with candied clementine and baked until golden (in a popover pan! I don't have baba molds—do you?!), then doused in a hot candied clementine syrup steeped with 44 coffee beans enhanced with a healthy amount of rum.

Makes 8 babas

For the Babas

75 mL (6 Tbsp) whole milk

210 g (1½ cups) all-purpose flour

1 Tbsp sugar

8 g (1 sachet/2¼ tsp) instant yeast

½ tsp salt

2 eggs, at room temperature

77 g (⅓ cup) unsalted butter, at room temperature

60 g (¼ cup) diced candied clementine wedges (page 25)

To make the babas, in a small saucepan or the microwave, warm the milk to just warm, 100°F to 110°F (38°C to 43°C). Set aside.

In the bowl of a stand mixer, combine the flour, sugar, yeast, and salt. Fit the mixer with the dough hook, add the warmed milk and eggs, and mix on low speed until combined. Increase the speed to medium and let the mixer knead the dough for 5 to 10 minutes, until the dough is smooth and elastic. Add the butter 1 tablespoon at a time, then mix in the candied clementine until incorporated. Let the dough rest for 10 minutes at room temperature.

Meanwhile, grease an eight-cavity popover pan.

Once the dough is done resting, use a 1½ oz ice cream scoop to portion 3 tablespoons of dough into each cavity of the popover pan. Cover with plastic wrap and let rise in a warm place until the dough doubles in size, about 30 minutes.

Preheat the oven to 375°F (190°C). Remove from the plastic wrap and bake the babas for 15 to 20 minutes, until golden brown and an instant-read thermometer inserted in the center reads 210°F (99°C). Meanwhile, make the syrup.

continued

For the Syrup

625 mL (2½ cups) candied clementine syrup (page 25 or 33)

44 coffee beans

190 mL (¾ cup) dark rum

For Serving

250 mL (1 cup) whipping cream

1 Tbsp icing sugar

2 tsp instant coffee

Candied orange or clementine wedges (page 25 or 33), for garnish (optional)

SIMPLIFY *Omit the candied clementine and make syrup by combining 450 g (2¼ cups) sugar, 250 mL (1 cup) water, the zest of one orange, and 190 mL (¾ cup) fresh-squeezed orange juice in a small pot and boiling until the sugar has dissolved.*

SUBSTITUTE *No clementine? Use candied Seville or navel orange peel and syrup (page 33). If you don't have a popover pan, divide the batter evenly in a standard 12-cup muffin tin and bake as directed.*

To make the syrup, in a medium saucepan, bring the clementine syrup and coffee beans to a boil. As soon as it comes to a boil, remove from the heat and let steep while you assemble the babas.

When the babas are ready, immediately remove them from the popover pan and transfer to an 8-inch square pan. Add the rum to the hot syrup and pour evenly over the babas. Let the babas sit for 10 minutes, then gently turn them and allow them to sit another 10 minutes.

To serve, in the bowl of a stand mixer fitted with the whisk attachment, whip the cream with the icing sugar and instant coffee until it holds firm peaks.

Serve warm, cold, or at room temperature with the coffee whipped cream. Garnish with candied orange or clementine, if desired.

Babas will keep, covered, at room temperature or in the refrigerator for up to 3 days.

COOKIE
JAR

WELSH
MOUNTAIN
PONIES

Welsh
3 c. flour
1 1/2 tsp. b. p
1/2 tsp. salt
1 tsp. soda
1 c. sug

Welsh Cakes

What are Welsh cakes? Honestly, I'm not sure. My granny served them most often from a decorative tin lined with waxed paper that had been squirreled away in the freezer. Since this was how she usually served cookies, I've always thought of Welsh cakes in that category, but my spouse considers them to be more in the family of scones—and then, of course, there's the fact that they're called cakes. Either way, they are the flavor of my childhood and one of my most favorite treats, made all the more special because none of the kids I knew had ever heard of them.

As with most family recipes, especially the specialties of those now departed, this one was a bit of work to decode. I found a handwritten recipe in my grandmother's script, but it just wasn't right when I made it. A text to my aunt confirmed that it wasn't the recipe my granny used at all! With a little guidance from said aunt, however, I think I managed to recapture this beloved cookie-scone hybrid of my youth, featuring my granny's special touches of candied peel and extra spice mixed into the coating sugar.

Makes 20 cakes

---

210 g (1½ cups) all-purpose flour

200 g (1 cup) sugar, divided

1 tsp freshly grated nutmeg, divided

½ tsp baking powder

½ tsp salt

⅛ tsp ground mace (optional)

58 g (¼ cup) lard or shortening, cold, cubed

58 g (¼ cup) unsalted butter, cold, cubed, plus more for frying

50 g (⅓ cup) currants

2 Tbsp minced candied orange peel (page 33)

1 egg, beaten

30–45 mL (2–3 Tbsp) whole milk

To begin, in a medium bowl, combine the flour, 100 g (½ cup) sugar, ½ teaspoon nutmeg, baking powder, salt, and mace, if using. Add the lard and butter and use your fingers to rub it in until the mixture resembles coarse crumbs. Stir in the currants and peel.

In a measuring cup, combine the egg and 2 tablespoons milk, then pour into the flour mixture. Stir until a pliable dough forms and has no dry bits. If it's too dry, add up to 1 tablespoon of additional milk. Alternatively, if the dough is too soft, chill in the refrigerator for 10 to 15 minutes to firm up.

On a lightly floured work surface, pat down the dough, dust with flour, and roll out to ¼ inch thick. Cut into 20 rounds using a 2¼-inch cutter (preferably fluted). You will need to gather the scraps and roll out again to get the 20.

continued

In a small bowl, combine the remaining sugar and nutmeg. Set a wire rack over a rimmed baking sheet. Set aside.

To cook, heat a griddle or large skillet over medium heat and grease modestly with butter. In batches, cook the Welsh cakes, leaving at least ½ inch of space between them, until golden brown, 2 to 3 minutes per side.

When the cakes are ready, transfer one at a time to the sugar-nutmeg mixture and coat with sugar on both sides. Transfer to the prepared wire rack to cool. Serve warm or at room temperature.

The Welsh cakes will keep in an airtight container at room temperature for up to 3 days or in the freezer for up to 3 months.

SIMPLIFY *Omit the candied peel and you've still got a pretty traditional Welsh cake.*

SUBSTITUTE *No currants? Use raisins or dried cranberries.*

Fruitcake Cookies

If you've run out of time to make and age fruitcakes this year, you're certainly not alone. Not to worry—these tender cookies pack in all of the flavors of a top-notch fruitcake, without the need to plan more than a night ahead, feed anything regularly with booze or to find cheesecloth at the supermarket. In fact, these delectable cookies are so good and capable of winning over any fruitcake skeptics, you should make them even if you've also made your aged fruitcake. If you are a such a planner, get ahead on holiday baking by freezing these after portioning and rolling in sugar. Note: You will need to start this recipe the night before.

Makes 30 cookies

---

85 g (⅓ cup) diced candied peel (page 33)

40 g (¼ cup) golden raisins

40 g (¼ cup) currants

36 g (¼ cup) dried cranberries

60 mL (¼ cup) brandy, dark rum, or orange juice

315 g (2¼ cups) all-purpose flour

1½ Tbsp Mixed Spice (page 196)

2 tsp baking soda

½ tsp salt

165 mL (⅔ cup) neutral oil

110 g (½ cup) brown sugar

100 g (½ cup) sugar, plus more for rolling

Zest of 1 orange

1 egg

The night before you make the fruitcake cookies, in a small bowl, combine the candied peel, raisins, currants, and dried cranberries with the brandy. Cover and let sit overnight, stirring once or twice.

The next day, preheat the oven to 350°F (175°C). Line two large rimmed baking sheets with parchment paper.

In a small bowl, whisk the flour, mixed spice, baking soda, and salt.

In a medium bowl, whisk the oil, both sugars, and orange zest until combined. Whisk in the egg, followed by the molasses.

continued

80 g (¼ cup) molasses

80 g (⅔ cup) chopped toasted nuts (preferably a mix of Brazil and pecan)

115 g (4 oz) crumbled marzipan (optional)

Fold the dry ingredients into the wet until almost combined. Fold in the soaked fruit mixture (including any liquid), nuts, and marzipan, if using, until well combined. Portion the dough using a 1 oz ice cream scoop to form 30 balls (about 2 tablespoons each), then roll the balls in sugar to coat. Place on the prepared baking sheets spaced 2 inches apart. (At this point you can freeze the unbaked dough. Just freeze on the baking sheet until the dough is solid and then transfer to an airtight container or freezer bag. They will keep in the freezer for at least 3 months.)

Bake the cookies, one sheet at a time, for 12 to 14 minutes, until the cookies are cracked and puffed. (If baking from frozen, add a few minutes to the baking time.) Cool completely on a wire rack.

The cookies will keep in an airtight container at room temperature for up to 1 week.

1. Star Anise & Candied Peel Sablé (page 117)
2. Chi's Spicy Strawberry Margarita Cookie (page 118)
3. Brown Butter Grapefruit Madeleine (page 130)

4. Cherry Hazelnut Ball (page 126)
5. Brown Butter Biscotti (page 114)
6. My Ideal Oatmeal Cookie (page 116)
7. Fruitcake Cookie (page 111)

Brown Butter Biscotti with Dates, Orange & Pecans

I love these. The nutty trifecta of brown butter, rye flour, and toasted pecans in this cookie is the perfect base note for caramelly dates and a bittersweet pop of candied orange peel. But to be honest, I was never much of a biscotti fan—until I tried the short, stout version at the magical (but now shuttered) Vergennes Laundry in Vermont. Bursting with nuts and dried fruit, they were good keepers but still tender. I was sold. But I really bought the farm once I adapted their recipe to incorporate one of my favorite flavor combinations—date, orange, and pecan—inspired by Big Sur Bakery (yes this is a mash-up remix).

Makes about 30 biscotti

---

140 g (1 cup) all-purpose flour

105 g (¾ cup) rye flour

1½ tsp baking powder

¾ tsp salt

85 g (6 Tbsp) Brown Butter (page 192), at room temperature

175 g (¾ cup + 2 Tbsp) sugar

1 egg

1 egg yolk

200 g (1 cup) pitted soft dates, roughly chopped

130 g (½ cup) diced candied orange peel (page 33)

85 g (¾ cup) toasted pecans

To begin, preheat the oven to 325°F (160°C). Line a large rimmed baking sheet with parchment paper.

In a small bowl, whisk the all-purpose and rye flours, baking powder, and salt. Set aside.

In the bowl of a stand mixer fitted with the paddle attachment, cream the brown butter and sugar on medium speed until smooth. Beat in the egg, followed by the egg yolk.

Add the flour mixture and mix on low speed until almost fully incorporated. Add the dates, diced candied peel, and pecans and mix until combined.

To bake, divide the dough in half and transfer to the prepared baking sheet. Form each piece into a log 2 inches wide and 12 inches long. Bake until the logs are puffed, set, and beginning to take on color, 30 to 35 minutes.

Transfer to a wire rack and let cool for 10 to 15 minutes.

Once cool enough to touch, transfer the baked logs to a cutting board. Using a serrated knife, slice each diagonally into ½-inch-thick slices. Arrange the biscotti on the prepared baking sheet (no need to space), return to the oven, and bake until lightly browned, 15 to 20 minutes.

Cool completely on the wire rack before storing in an airtight container at room temperature. They will keep for at least 2 weeks.

Recipe pictured on page 113

My Ideal Oatmeal Cookies

I insisted on these cookies at a bakery where I was once the pastry chef, even though they were a lot of work to make and didn't sell particularly well. I get it—oatmeal cookies are perhaps not as sexy as the ones next to them with the pools of melted dark chocolate—but these are SO GOOD. And if you already have candied peel on hand, they're not too much work at all. Originally these were made with a more labor-intensive brown butter, but I've given you a break here—though you can go all the way if you feel like it.

Makes 16 cookies

---

145 g (½ cup + 2 Tbsp) unsalted butter, at room temperature

110 g (½ cup) brown sugar

100 g (½ cup) sugar

1 egg

1 tsp vanilla extract

175 g (1¼ cups) all-purpose flour

½ tsp baking soda

½ tsp salt

¼ tsp baking powder

180 g (1½ cups) old-fashioned rolled oats

75 g (2½ oz) chopped blonde chocolate (preferably Valrhona Dulcey)

60 g (½ cup) toasted walnut pieces

50 g (3 Tbsp) diced candied citrus peel (page 33)

40 g (¼ cup) currants

Flaky salt, for sprinkling

Recipe pictured on page 113

To begin, preheat the oven to 350°F (175°C). Line two rimmed baking sheets with parchment paper.

In the bowl of a stand mixer fitted with the paddle attachment, cream the butter and both sugars. Beat in the egg, followed by the vanilla. Add the flour, baking soda, salt, and baking powder and mix just until combined. Add the oats, chocolate, walnuts, candied citrus peel, and currants and mix until combined.

Portion the dough using a 1½ oz ice cream scoop (about 3 tablespoons each) and place 2 inches apart onto the prepared baking sheets. Flatten the dough a little with your moistened palm. (At this point you can freeze the unbaked dough. Just transfer the dough to a small waxed paper–lined rimmed baking sheet, freeze until solid, and transfer to a resealable plastic bag or airtight container. Simply bake from frozen, which may take a few minutes longer.)

To bake, sprinkle with flaky salt. Bake, one sheet at a time, for 12 to 15 minutes, until light golden brown. Cool on a wire rack. The cookies will keep in an airtight container at room temperature for up to 3 days.

SIMPLIFY *Omit the candied peel and use the zest of one orange instead, adding it at the creaming stage at the beginning of the recipe.*

Star Anise & Candied Peel Sablés

The love-it-or-hate-it combo of licorice and orange has been a favorite of mine ever since discovering tiger ice cream as a kid. I've made a marmalade, a pound cake, and now a buttery slice-and-bake cookie. If you're in the hate-it camp, however, just substitute your favorite spice and candied fruit.

Makes 48 sablés

---

230 g (1 cup) unsalted butter, at room temperature

150 g (¾ cup) sugar

2 egg yolks

280 g (2 cups) all-purpose flour

1½ tsp ground star anise

½ tsp salt

130 g (½ cup) diced candied Seville orange or pink grapefruit peel (page 33)

SIMPLIFY *Omit candied peel or use dried fruit (page 60) instead.*

SUBSTITUTE *No candied peel and star anise? Use candied pineapple (page 25) and cardamom, candied cranberries (page 39) and minced fresh rosemary, or candied cherries (page 25 or 28) and seeds from a vanilla bean.*

Recipe pictured on page 113

To begin, in the bowl of a stand mixer fitted with the paddle attachment, beat the butter on low speed until creamy. Add the sugar and increase the speed to medium until blended (no need to whip!). Add the egg yolks and beat just until combined.

Reduce the speed to low and gradually add the flour, star anise, and salt and mix until just combined. Remove the paddle and use a spatula to fold in the candied peel.

Divide the dough into two equal portions. Place each portion on a piece of parchment or waxed paper and roll into logs 2 inches in diameter and 9 inches long. Twist up the ends of the paper to seal and place the logs in the freezer for at least 2 hours or place the wrapped logs in a freezer bag to store up to 2 months.

When ready to bake, preheat the oven to 350°F (175°C). Line two baking sheets with parchment paper. Remove the logs from the freezer, unwrap, and slice each log into ⅓-inch rounds (you should have 48).

Place the rounds 1 inch apart on the prepared baking sheets and bake for 15 to 18 minutes, turning once, until golden and firm.

Cool completely on a wire rack. The cookies will keep in an airtight container at room temperature for up to 1 week.

Chi's Spicy Strawberry Margarita Cookies

I adored Chi Nguyễn before we ever met—from watching them on television! Chi was a finalist on season 6 of *The Great Canadian Baking Show* (and the first openly non-binary contestant). They made it to the finale, spotlighting the flavors of their childhood to decolonize Eurocentric approaches to baking. Cooking competition shows usually stress me out, but this Canadian adaptation of *The Great British Bake-Off* is so sweet, and my partner and I were rooting for Chi every Sunday night. Happily, it turned out we both live in Toronto, so we became Internet friends and then IRL friends. An incredibly generous person, Chi shared cookie boxes with a bunch of bakers over the holidays, and no one could stop talking about these ones in particular, so I asked them if I could share the recipe with the world. The candied jalapeños and togarashi add heat and texture, while the freeze-dried strawberries bring brightness. As a finishing touch, the cookies are rolled in a mouth-puckering sour sugar coating. From the first bite to the last, these are a little summertime dance party even during the coldest of winter nights.

Makes 30 cookies

---

230 g (1 cup) unsalted butter,
    at room temperature

350 g (1¾ cups) sugar

1 egg, at room temperature

1 egg yolk, at room temperature

2 tsp vanilla extract

2 tsp salt

Zest of 1 lime

360 g (2½ cups + 1 Tbsp)
    all-purpose flour

1 tsp baking soda

½ tsp cream of tartar

2 tsp shichimi togarashi or any
    other red chili pepper powder,
    like gochugaru

To prepare the cookies, preheat the oven to 350°F (175°C) and line a rimmed baking sheet with parchment paper.

In the bowl of a stand mixer fitted with the paddle attachment, cream the butter on medium speed until softened. Add the sugar and mix on medium speed, scraping down the sides of the bowl at least two to three times, until pale yellow, about 5 minutes. Add the egg, egg yolk, vanilla, salt, and lime zest. Mix on medium speed for 1 minute, until combined. Add the flour, baking soda, cream of tartar, and shichimi togarashi. Mix on medium speed for 30 seconds. Add the candied jalapeños and freeze-dried strawberries. Mix on low for 30 seconds, then increase the speed to medium until the dough just comes together and pulls away from the sides of the bowl.

100 g (1 cup) dried and sugared
    candied jalapeños (page 25),
    roughly diced
30 g (1¼ cups) freeze-dried
    strawberries, roughly crushed
50 g (¼ cup) superfine sugar
1 tsp citric acid

Use a ¾ oz (1½-tablespoon) scoop or measure out 35 g balls of cookie dough to portion the dough.

In a small bowl, combine the superfine sugar and citric acid. Roll each cookie in the sour sugar mixture and place on the prepared baking sheet 2 inches apart. (At this point you can freeze the unbaked dough. Just freeze on the baking sheet until the dough is solid, then transfer to an airtight container or freezer bag. The dough will keep in the freezer for at least 3 months.)

Bake until the cookies are golden brown on the edges and puffed in the center, 11 to 13 minutes. (If baking from frozen, you will need to add a few more minutes to the baking time.)

To finish, cool on the pans for 5 minutes before transferring to a wire rack. If you want perfect round circles, use a drinking glass or a round cookie cutter to gently coax and shape the cookies right after taking them out of the oven, while they are still piping hot.

The cookies will keep in an airtight container at room temperature for up to 4 days.

Recipe pictured on page 113

Banana Split Blondies

I've got a real soft spot for banana splits. My dad always used to take me out for one at Burger King in the summer and we'd eat it at a picnic table. The decadence of its size, the novelty of fresh fruit in a fast-food dish, the acid-bittersweet trifecta of pineapple, chocolate, and strawberry sauce against the creamy soft serve—what dreams are made of! It's all reimagined here as a banana and white chocolate blondie chock-full of candied pineapple and cherries and toasted walnuts, swirled with strawberry jam, drizzled with chocolate, and finished with sprinkles and more banana, be it freeze-dried or chips. Doctor it up for dessert, as in the photo, with lightly sweetened whipped cream, fresh banana, and (of course) a candied cherry on top. Put the rest in your purse to be instantly transported when necessary.

Makes 16 blondies

---

115 g (½ cup) unsalted butter

90 g (3 oz) white chocolate

146 g (⅔ cup) brown sugar

1 egg

125 g (½ cup) mashed ripe banana

1½ tsp vanilla extract

140 g (1 cup) all-purpose flour

1 tsp baking powder

½ tsp salt

60 g (¼ cup) diced candied pineapple (page 25)

60 g (½ cup) toasted walnut pieces

55 g (¼ cup) chopped candied cherries (page 25 or 28)

80 g (¼ cup) strawberry jam

30 g (1 oz) dark chocolate

½ tsp neutral oil

To prepare the blondies, preheat the oven to 350°F (175°C). Grease an 8-inch square pan and line it with parchment paper.

In a heatproof bowl set over simmering water, or in the microwave in 30-second increments, melt the butter and white chocolate. Whisk in the brown sugar, followed by the egg. Stir in the mashed banana and vanilla. Add the flour, baking powder, and salt, stirring just until combined. Fold in the candied pineapple, walnuts, and candied cherries.

To bake the blondies, transfer the batter to the prepared pan, smoothing the top with a small offset spatula. Dollop with strawberry jam, then use the tip of a knife to swirl it in gently. Bake for 30 to 35 minutes, until golden brown and set. Let cool completely on a wire rack.

continued

Banana chips or freeze-dried banana, to garnish

Rainbow sprinkles, to garnish

To finish, in a heatproof bowl set over simmering water, or in the microwave in 30-second increments, melt the dark chocolate with the oil. Drizzle over top the cooled blondie, then sprinkle with banana chips and rainbow sprinkles. Refrigerate until set, about 10 minutes. Cut into 16 squares. Alternatively you can cut into 9 squares and then cut each in half diagonally to make 18 wedges. The blondies will keep in an airtight container at room temperature for up to 5 days.

SIMPLIFY *Use store-bought candied or dried pineapple and dried cherries or Amarena cherries in place of homemade.*

Mendiant Shortbread

This chocolate shortbread is glorious topped with rich crème fraîche ganache, but once you decorate it with the perfect pattern of candied and dried fruits, nuts, and whatever else your heart desires, I'm sorry to say it's almost too stunning to cut into. All the more reason to make this jumbo homage to the classic French chocolate mendiant as a gift or the finale to a dinner party!

Makes 12 wedges

For the Shortbread

230 g (1 cup) unsalted butter, at room temperature

94 g (¾ cup) icing sugar

60 g (2 oz) dark chocolate, melted and cooled

245 g (1¾ cups) all-purpose flour

2 Tbsp cocoa powder

2 Tbsp cornstarch

1 tsp salt

For the Ganache

80 g (2¾ oz) dark chocolate callets

125 g (½ cup) crème fraîche

To Finish (mix and match)

Candied fruit, vegetables, and/or nuts (pages 56–57)

Dried fruit and nuts

Crystallized flowers and/or herbs (page 49)

Preheat the oven to 325°F (160°C). Grease a 9-inch tart pan with a removable bottom.

To make the shortbread, in a large bowl, cream the butter and icing sugar until silky. Blend in the melted chocolate. Sift in the flour, cocoa, cornstarch, and salt and stir until combined.

Transfer to the prepared tart pan and evenly spread the batter with a small offset spatula. Prick all over with a fork. Bake for 55 minutes to 1 hour and 10 minutes, until the shortbread is firm and set. Let cool completely on a wire rack.

To make the ganache, place the chocolate in a small heatproof bowl. In a small pot set over medium heat, bring the crème fraîche to a simmer. Immediately pour the crème fraîche over the chocolate and let sit for 1 minute.

Whisk until the chocolate has melted and the mixture is emulsified. Using an offset spatula, spread the crème fraîche–chocolate mixture evenly over the surface of the cooled shortbread.

continued

To finish, decorate the surface with candied and/or dried fruit and nuts, candied vegetables, crystallized flowers and/or herbs—whatever you desire. Allow the ganache to set before cutting. The shortbread will keep in an airtight container at room temperature for at least 5 days.

SIMPLIFY *No candied fruit? Just use dried fruit and nuts. This shortbread is also excellent unadorned or enhanced with just a sprinkle of flaky salt.*

SUBSTITUTE *No crème fraîche? Whipping cream works in a pinch. No dark chocolate? Make it with white chocolate. Just replace the cocoa with all-purpose flour and omit the dark chocolate from the shortbread. No dark chocolate callets for the ganache? Use white chocolate. You can also chill the dough, roll it out to ¼ inch thick, and cut out rounds to decorate as individual mendiant cookies. Reduce the baking time to 20 minutes.*

Cherry Hazelnut Balls

My granny used to make nut crescents, a typical European Christmas cookie, and I adored them. When I saw a variation in an old Czech cookbook to roll them into balls encasing a candied cherry, my imagination ran wild. Use this basic formula to concoct your dream cookie: use brandied cherries or add crushed freeze-dried cherries to the coating sugar to enhance the flavor and tease at what lies within. A caramelized or toasted nut or even a piece of chocolate makes an excellent center, but there are many substitutions (see right).

Makes 20 balls

---

115 g (½ cup) unsalted butter, at room temperature

50 g (3 Tbsp) sugar

1 egg yolk

1 tsp vanilla extract

187 g (1⅓ cups) all-purpose flour

35 g (⅓ cup) toasted ground hazelnuts

Scant ½ tsp salt

20 candied cherries (page 28), drained and patted dry if in syrup

200 g (1 cup) superfine vanilla sugar (see note)

SIMPLIFY *Use store-bought Amarena or maraschino cherries instead of candied.*

To prepare the balls, preheat the oven to 300°F (150°C). Line two baking sheets with parchment paper.

In a medium bowl, cream the butter and sugar. Beat in the yolk, followed by the vanilla. Stir in the flour, hazelnuts, and salt until well combined.

Flatten 1 level tablespoon of dough in the palm of your hand. Place a candied cherry in the center, then enclose in the dough. Roll between your palms to make a smooth sphere, then place on the prepared baking sheets. Repeat with the remaining dough and cherries, spacing the cookies 1 inch apart (you should have 20 balls).

To bake the balls, bake, one sheet at a time, for 25 to 30 minutes, until the balls are firm and the bottoms are golden. Immediately roll the balls in vanilla sugar to coat, then transfer to a wire rack to cool completely.

The balls will keep in an airtight container at room temperature for at least 1 week.

NOTE *Superfine vanilla sugar is available at the grocery store (Dr. Oetker has one) or rub the seeds from ½ vanilla bean into 1 cup superfine sugar.*

SUBSTITUTE *No hazelnuts? Use ground pistachios. No candied cherries? Use candied strawberries (page 28) and make a strawberry sugar (page 62) to roll them in by combining 94 g (¾ cup) icing sugar + 1 tablespoon freeze-dried strawberry powder.*

Sort of Sbrisolona

One of the great joys of working as a pastry cook is getting to eat errant bits of buttery, sandy streusel (aka the best part of a muffin). When I discovered the Italian cookie sbrisolona (made in Mantua since the 16th century!), which is basically a disk of baked streusel, I instantly fell in love. The combination of hazelnut, buckwheat, espresso, and candied grapefruit in this version might seem unusual, but I implore you to trust me.

Serves 12 to 16

---

200 g (1⅓ cups) toasted skinned hazelnuts, divided

140 g (1 cup) all-purpose flour

70 g (½ cup) buckwheat flour

133 g (⅔ cup) sugar

2 tsp ground espresso (decaf, if desired)

½ tsp salt

153 g (⅔ cup) unsalted butter, at room temperature

85 g (⅓ cup) diced candied pink grapefruit peel (page 33)

Icing sugar, for dusting (optional)

SUBSTITUTE *No hazelnuts? Try these nuts instead, replacing the buckwheat and candied grapefruit with other pairings blanched and toasted almonds, kamut flour, and candied orange peel; or whole toasted pecans, rye flour, and candied figs.*

To begin, preheat the oven to 350°F (175°C). Grease a 9-inch tart pan with a removable bottom (a springform pan works too).

In a food processor, pulse 150 g (1 cup) hazelnuts, the all-purpose and buckwheat flours, sugar, espresso, and salt until the nuts are finely ground. Add the butter and pulse until the butter is incorporated and the mixture resembles fine crumbs. Continue pulsing until large crumbs the size of olives begin to form. Transfer the crumb mixture to a bowl and fold in the remaining whole hazelnuts and candied peel.

Scatter the crumbs evenly into the prepared pan, pressing gently but not packing. Bake for 40 to 50 minutes, until firm and light golden brown. Place the pan on a wire rack and cool completely.

To serve, remove from the pan and dust with icing sugar, if desired. Either cut into wedges or, my preference, simply let guests break off pieces.

Sbrisolona will keep in an airtight container at room temperature for up to 1 week.

SIMPLIFY *Omit the candied peel or replace with dried fruit. Prunes would work especially well here.*

Brown Butter Grapefruit Madeleines

I didn't think I liked madeleines until I tried the ones at the fabulous Duchess Bake Shop in my hometown of Edmonton. I tried making my own, but I was never satisfied until I learned their technique of dunking the hot little cakes in syrup, which gives them a gorgeous texture and prolongs their shelf life. Now I can finally give my madeleine pans, which I purchased in pastry school but have barely used since, the workout they deserve.

Makes 12 madeleines

For the Madeleines

80 g (½ cup + 1 Tbsp) all-purpose flour

¼ tsp baking powder

¼ tsp salt

2 eggs

75 g (6 Tbsp) sugar

77 g (⅓ cup) Brown Butter, melted and cooled (page 192)

½ tsp vanilla extract

2 Tbsp diced candied grapefruit peel (page 33)

190 mL (¾ cup) candied grapefruit syrup (page 25 or 33)

To Finish

63 g (½ cup) icing sugar

1½ Tbsp Brown Butter (page 192), melted

1½ Tbsp grapefruit juice

½ tsp grapefruit zest

To begin, in a small bowl, whisk the flour, baking powder, and salt. Set aside.

In a medium bowl, whisk the eggs and sugar, then whisk in the brown butter and vanilla. Add the dry ingredients and mix to combine, then fold in the candied grapefruit peel. Place plastic wrap directly on the surface of the batter. Refrigerate for at least 3 hours and up to 3 days.

Preheat the oven to 400°F (200°C). Grease and flour a 12-cavity madeleine pan well—they can stick prodigiously! Using a piping bag fitted with a large plain tip, or simply a spoon, fill the cavities with the batter until they are three-quarters full.

Bake the madeleines for 10 to 12 minutes, until golden brown. They should have a distinctive hump in the middle. While the madeleines are baking, place the grapefruit syrup in a small bowl. Set a wire rack over a rimmed baking sheet. When the madeleines are ready, remove them from the oven, unmold, and immediately dip the hot madeleines in the syrup to coat. Transfer to the prepared wire rack to cool.

continued

To finish, in a small bowl, whisk the icing sugar, brown butter, grapefruit juice, and zest. Dip the scalloped side of the cooled madeleines in the glaze to coat, shaking off any excess glaze. Return to the wire rack to set.

Madeleines are best eaten the day they are made, but actually keep 2–3 days in an airtight container when given the syrup-dunking treatment.

SIMPLIFY *Omit the candied peel and add the zest of one grapefruit or 2 tablespoons chopped grapefruit marmalade to the batter with the sugar. Omit the candied grapefruit syrup and make simple syrup (page 197) instead, flavored with grapefruit zest and/or liqueur to taste.*

SUBSTITUTE *No candied grapefruit peel and syrup? Use any candied fruit and its syrup that you desire— stem ginger (page 33), kumquat (pages 56–57), cranberry (page 39), Buddha's hand (pages 56–57). No brown butter? Use regular unsalted. You can also replace the brown butter in the glaze with additional grapefruit juice.*

Candied Fig & Walnut Baklava

In a bid to make more use of the fragrant, pale violet syrup left over from candying figs, this Ottoman delicacy, baklava, came to mind. It makes a delightful hissing sound when you pour the cold syrup, doctored with just a little lemon and vanilla, over the hot pan of crisp, buttery layers of phyllo pastry sandwiching rich walnuts and succulent candied figs. Much less delightful is the torturous wait for it to cool down until you can eat it. But it's worth the wait.

Makes 42 baklavas

---

350 g (2½ cups) finely chopped walnuts

½ tsp cinnamon

½ tsp salt

¼ tsp ground cloves

454 g (1 lb) phyllo pastry

230 g (1 cup) unsalted butter, melted

190 g drained candied figs (about 3) (page 28) (reserving syrup), sliced ¼ inch thick

440 mL (1¾ cups) reserved candied fig syrup (page 28)

45 mL (3 Tbsp lemon juice)

1 tsp vanilla extract

Flaky salt, for sprinkling

To begin, preheat the oven to 350°F (175°C). Grease a 9 × 13-inch pan.

In a medium bowl, toss together the nuts, cinnamon, salt, and cloves.

Unroll the phyllo pastry on the counter and use a sharp knife to cut it in half crosswise so that it fits the pan (if your phyllo is a different shape, trim it however you need to fit the pan). Keeping the two halves separate, cover with a clean, damp tea towel to keep it from drying out.

Place one sheet of phyllo in the bottom of the pan and brush with melted butter. Repeat until half of the phyllo is used up. Add two-thirds of the nut mixture in an even layer on top of the phyllo, then top evenly with the fig slices. Place a layer of phyllo on top and brush with butter. Repeat until half of the remaining phyllo is used up. Add the remaining nut mixture in an even layer on top, then top with the remaining phyllo, a layer at a time, brushing with butter as you go. Refrigerate until firm, about 15 minutes.

continued

To finish, making sure to cut all the way to the bottom, use a sharp knife to cut the baklava diagonally into six strips one way and then six strips the other way to make diamonds. Make five cuts parallel to the short edge of the pan, bisecting the diamonds to create triangles. You should have about 42 pieces roughly the same size. Bake until the baklavas are a deep golden brown, 45 to 55 minutes.

Meanwhile, in a large measuring cup, whisk the fig syrup, lemon juice, and vanilla. Refrigerate until ready to use.

When the baklavas are ready, transfer to a wire rack and immediately carefully pour the syrup all over. Sprinkle with flaky salt. Let cool completely before serving.

The baklavas will keep, covered, at room temperature for up to 2 weeks.

CANDY
BOX

Left to Right:
Mendiants (see right),
Kumquat Pecan Pralines (page 140),
Torrone Mallows (page 141), and
Chestnut Truffles (page 143)

Mendiants

Mendiants are a simple, classic chocolate, and I especially love how maximally customizable they are. They're easy once you've got the hang of tempering chocolate—just decorate little rounds of chocolate as though they were a canvas, then let them set. You can use dried (page 59), glazed (page 60), or sugared (page 60) candied fruits, toasted or candied nuts or coconut (page 44), crystallized flowers and herbs (page 49), dried fruits, or a combination of them all. Go classic with candied pistachios, dried apricot slivers, and candied orange peel, or get a little weird with an all-candied vegetable version. Dark, milk, or white chocolate are classic, but don't forget about blonde or fruit-flavored chocolate. This recipe uses 200 g (7 oz) chocolate. Adjust the quantity to temper enough chocolate for the number of mendiants you want to make.

Makes twelve 2¼-inch mendiants

---

200 g (7 oz) chocolate

***To Finish (mix and match,
all finished as desired)***
Candied and/or dried fruit
(pages 56–57)
Candied coconut (page 44)
Candied and/or toasted nuts
(page 47)
Candied vegetables (page 19)
Crystallized flowers and/or herbs
(page 49)

To begin, line a baking sheet with parchment paper or a silicone mat. Temper the chocolate (page 64), then dollop the chocolate onto the prepared sheet, leaving a bit of room for spread.

To finish, decorate with your desired finishings and allow to set, about 30 minutes to 1 hour.

The mendiants will keep in an airtight container at cool room temperature for at least 1 month.

Kumquat Pecan Pralines

Candy within a candy?! What is this, Hamlet's Confectionery? Every year at Christmas I make a ton of cookies and candies to eat and share, always a mix of new recipes and old standbys we can't do without—like these pralines, which must show up every single year without fail. They remind me so much of one of my favorite sweets as a kid: toffee from my grandmother's recipe. It was impossible to replicate, and my mom would sometimes (but not reliably) screw it up so that it was slightly grainy and totally melt in the mouth. When I first made the pralines this recipe was developed from, I felt such joy at rediscovering that transcendent texture. The kumquats bring some brightness to keep the sublime richness in check.

Makes 21 pralines

---

330 g (1½ cups) brown sugar

190 mL (¾ cup) heavy cream

150 g (¾ cup) sugar

87 g (6 Tbsp) unsalted butter

180 g (1½ cups) toasted pecans

60 g (¼ cup) diced dried candied kumquats (page 25)

¾ tsp salt

1 tsp vanilla extract

1 Tbsp whisky (preferably rye)

SIMPLIFY *Omit the candied kumquats and use 1 tablespoon orange zest instead (but add a couple extra tablespoons of pecans). If you don't like the whisky, simply omit.*

SUBSTITUTE *No candied kumquats? Use your favorite candied citrus (page 28) or even cranberries (page 39).*

To begin, line a large baking sheet with parchment paper.

In a medium pot over medium-high heat, combine the brown sugar, cream, sugar, and butter. Cook, stirring occasionally, until the mixture reaches 230°F (110°C). Stir in the pecans, kumquats, and salt. Cook until the mixture reaches 240°F (116°C). Remove from the heat, add the vanilla, and transfer the mixture to a heatproof bowl. Let sit undisturbed until the mixture cools to 210°F (99°C), about 10 minutes. Add the whisky, then use a spatula or wooden spoon to stir the mixture until it thickens and becomes opaque.

To finish, use a 1 oz scoop (or scoop 2 tablespoons) to portion the mixture onto the prepared sheet, spacing the pralines 1 inch apart (you should have 21 pieces). Let cool completely at room temperature before serving.

The pralines will keep in an airtight container at room temperature for at least 1 week.

Recipe pictured on page 130

Torrone Mallows

This is another fantastic recipe courtesy of the illustrious Michelle Marek (page 93). To the average person, this is a delicious (and egg-free) homemade marshmallow made extra enticing with the addition of honey, dark chocolate, orange, pistachios, and espresso. To the pastry chef, this is a delicious treat too, but also kind of a practical joke because it looks and tastes like another classic treat, nougat, though with a totally different texture—much more yielding and meltable. So think of it as a delicious addition to a candy box or hot chocolate (omitting the nuts for the latter), and maybe as a funny *trompe l'oeil*; it cracked Michelle up so much she created it! Note: You will want to start this the night before.

Makes sixty-four 1-inch marshmallows

---

65 g (⅓ cup + 1 Tbsp) pistachios

2 Tbsp diced candied orange peel (page 33)

20 g (10 sheets) gelatin, soaked and drained

½ Tbsp ground espresso

1 tsp vanilla extract

Zest of 1 orange

Pinch of salt

400 g (2 cups) sugar

85 g (¼ cup) honey

60 g (2 oz) dark chocolate, melted

63 g (½ cup) icing sugar

64 g (½ cup) cornstarch

To begin, grease an 8-inch square pan and line with parchment paper, then grease the parchment.

In the bowl of a stand mixer fitted with the whisk attachment, combine the pistachios, candied orange peel, gelatin, espresso, vanilla, orange zest, and salt.

In a small pot, combine the sugar, honey, and 125 mL (½ cup) water. Bring to a boil over medium-high heat, stirring occasionally to dissolve the sugar. Heat to 240°F (116°C).

Remove from the heat and, with the mixer running on low, slowly pour the syrup into the bowl of the stand mixer. Increase the speed to medium-high and whip until the mixture is billowy white and almost cool.

Remove the whisk and quickly but gently fold in half of the melted chocolate for a marble effect, being careful not to overmix. Transfer to the prepared pan and swirl the remaining chocolate onto the surface of the marshmallow. Let sit overnight, uncovered, at room temperature.

continued

To finish, in a medium bowl, combine the icing sugar and cornstarch.

Using a knife, which may need to be oiled, cut the marshmallows into 1-inch squares or whatever size you prefer. (You should have 64 marshmallows unless you choose a different size.)

Toss the marshmallows in the icing sugar mixture and then store in an airtight container. They will keep at room temperature for at least 2 weeks.

Recipe pictured on page 130

Chestnut Truffles

The nutty, buttery, earthy flavor of smooth chestnut purée plays very, very well with dark chocolate and rum in these melt-in-your-mouth truffles studded with candied chestnut pieces. Note: You will want to start this the night before.

Makes 40 truffles

---

56 g (⅓ cup) diced candied chestnuts (page 28 or 33)

1½ Tbsp dark rum

200 g (7 oz) dark chocolate callets

200 g (⅔ cup) chestnut cream

170 g (⅔ cup) crème fraîche

1 Tbsp unsalted butter

¼ tsp flaky salt

55 g (½ cup) cocoa powder

To begin, grease a 5 × 9-inch loaf pan and line with parchment paper.

In a small bowl, combine the candied chestnuts and rum. Set aside.

In a heatproof bowl, combine the chocolate, chestnut cream, crème fraîche, butter, and salt. Set the bowl over a pan of simmering water or in the microwave for 30-second bursts. Stirring often, heat until the chocolate melts and the mixture is homogeneous. If it begins to look broken, whisk it vigorously until glossy.

Stir in the candied chestnuts and rum mixture. Pour into the prepared pan, spreading the mixture evenly with an offset spatula or knife. Refrigerate overnight.

To finish, place the cocoa powder in a shallow bowl. Unmold the truffle slab from the pan and peel off the parchment. Cut into 40 squares (4 strips lengthwise by 10 crosswise).

Toss the truffles in the cocoa powder, shaking off any excess. Serve immediately or store in an airtight container in the refrigerator for up to 2 weeks or in the freezer for up to 2 months.

Recipe pictured on page 130

SIMPLIFY *Omit the candied chestnuts.*

Ginger Cashew Caramel Corn

Spicy candied ginger brings intrigue to this buttery, perfectly salted, crispy caramel corn (the last thanks to the baking soda). Bag it up for gifts or slowly whittle down your supply while watching prestige television.

Makes 1 kg (2.2 lb)

2 Tbsp ghee (optional)

130 g (12 cups) popped popcorn or 100 g (½ cup) kernels

156 g (1 cup) salted roasted cashews

105 g (⅔ cup) diced dried candied ginger (page 28 or 33)

1½ Tbsp salt

1½ tsp baking soda

1 tsp ground ginger

400 g (2 cups) sugar

125 mL (½ cup) ginger syrup (page 28 and 33)

60 mL (¼ cup) light corn syrup

58 g (¼ cup) unsalted butter

SUBSTITUTE *No candied ginger? Replace with candied pineapple (page 25), candied coconut chips (page 44) in place of cashews, and the zest of one lime in place of the ground ginger.*

If you have popped popcorn ready to go, move onto the next step.

Otherwise, to make the popcorn from scratch, in a large pot over medium-high heat, add the ghee and three kernels. Once those pop, add the remaining kernels, reduce the heat to medium, and crack the lid a little. Cook, shaking the pot occasionally, until the popping ceases. You should have 130 g (12 cups) of popped popcorn. Set aside.

Line a large baking sheet (or two smaller ones) with parchment paper. Grease a large bowl with butter, then add the popcorn, cashews, and candied ginger.

In a small bowl, combine the salt, baking soda, and ground ginger. Set aside.

In a medium pot, combine the sugar, ginger syrup, corn syrup, and butter. Bring to a boil over medium-high heat without stirring (though feel free to swirl the pot occasionally). Cook until the mixture turns medium amber, then remove from the heat and quickly whisk in the reserved salt mixture. It will bubble prodigiously!

To finish, immediately pour the caramel over the popcorn and mix quickly and thoroughly, making sure everything is well coated. Spread onto the prepared baking sheet and allow to cool completely. Once cool, break the caramel corn into pieces and store in an airtight container. It will keep for about 2 weeks.

SIMPLIFY *Instead of the candied ginger and syrup, you can use store-bought candied ginger, replace the syrup with more corn syrup, and increase the ground ginger to 1 tablespoon.*

PUDDINGS
& PIES

Candied Citron & Apple Tartlets Tatin

This recipe contains multitudes! Though the classic tarte tatin—caramelized apples topped with puff pastry and baked upside down—intimidates most bakers, this could scarcely be easier. Instead of dubious store-bought or labor-intensive homemade puff pastry, an easy cream cheese dough does the job equally well, while a slice of candied citron capping the apple looks impressive and cuts the sugar with a hint of bitterness. Serve with a dollop of whipped cream and let the compliments roll in.

Makes 8 tartlets

For the Pastry

140 g (1 cup) all-purpose flour

115 g (½ cup) unsalted butter, cold, cubed

115 g (4 oz) cream cheese, cold, cubed

¼ tsp salt

For the Tartlets

4 apples (preferably Ginger Gold or Mutsu)

58 g (¼ cup) unsalted butter, divided

100 g (½ cup) sugar, divided, plus more for sprinkling

8 candied citron slices (page 28)

To make the pastry, in the bowl of a stand mixer fitted with the paddle attachment, mix the flour, butter, cream cheese, and salt on medium-low speed until the dough comes together in a rough mass. Form into a disk, wrap, and chill in the refrigerator for at least 30 minutes. (Or freeze for up to 1 month and bring to cool room temperature before using.)

On a lightly floured surface, roll the dough to ⅓ inch thick and cut out eight 4-inch rounds (you will need to reroll the scraps). Freeze the rounds, separated by layers of parchment paper, until solid, at least 2 hours.

To make the tartlets, preheat the oven to 425°F (220°C). Grease eight large muffin cups or mini pie plates and set them on a rimmed baking sheet.

Peel and halve the apples. Use a melon baller or teaspoon to remove the core. Place ½ tablespoon butter and 1 tablespoon sugar in the bottom of each muffin cup. Top with a round of candied citron, followed by an apple half, core facing up. Sprinkle ½ to ¾ teaspoon sugar into the cavity. Top with a frozen pastry round.

continued

Bake for 25 to 35 minutes, until the pastry is golden brown and the apple is very tender.

Wait a few minutes before carefully inverting them onto a serving platter.

These are best enjoyed the day they are made, accompanied by some whipped cream. They can also be made a few hours ahead; just reheat in a 400°F (200°C) oven for 5 to 10 minutes, until the caramel is bubbling.

SIMPLIFY *No candied citron? Simply omit for a classic mini tarte tatin.*

SUBSTITUTE *No candied citron? Use candied lemon slices (page 28).*

Nesselrode Pie

This old-school chiffon pie is basically extinct, but I'm hoping we can bring it back. It's one of the many desserts that fall under the Nesselrode umbrella, which all contain candied fruit, booze, and often chestnut. The original form was an ice cream bombe created for a Russian count by Antonin Carême in the early 19th century. The pie version, originally created around 1940 by NYC baker Hortense Spier, has had many iterations, including a 1950s-style boxed cake mix with subpar candied fruit, which is likely partially responsible for its demise. This version, with its airy rum-laced filling and Della Robbia wreath–like décor, certainly deserves a second chance.

Serves 8 to 10

For the Crust

180 g (1½ cups) fine chocolate cookie crumbs

77 g (⅓ cup) unsalted butter, melted

¼ tsp salt

For the Filling

160 g (⅔ cup) mixed diced candied fruits (pages 56–57)

45 mL (3 Tbsp) dark rum

3 eggs, separated

88 g (7 Tbsp) sugar, divided

1 Tbsp cornstarch

1 tsp vanilla extract

375 mL (1½ cups) half and half

10 g (5 sheets) gelatin, softened

¼ tsp cream of tartar

¼ tsp salt

Preheat the oven to 375°F (190°C). Grease a 9-inch pie plate.

To make the crust, in a medium bowl, combine the crumbs, butter, and salt. Press evenly and firmly into the pie plate. Bake for 8 to 10 minutes, or until set. Cool completely on a wire rack.

To make the filling, in a small bowl, combine the candied fruits and rum. Set aside.

In a medium pot, whisk the egg yolks, 50 g (¼ cup) sugar, cornstarch, and vanilla. Gradually whisk in the half and half. Cook, stirring often, over medium heat, until the mixture comes to a boil. Remove from the heat, stir in the gelatin until it dissolves, then strain through a fine-mesh sieve into a large bowl. Let cool to room temperature, 1 to 2 hours (or speed up the process by stirring the mixture in an ice bath).

continued

To Finish

125 mL (½ cup) whipping cream

1 Tbsp icing sugar

Candied fruits (pages 56–57),
  to decorate

Marzipan fruits, to decorate
  (optional)

In the bowl of a stand mixer fitted with the whisk attachment, whip the egg whites with the cream of tartar and salt until foamy. Increase the speed to medium-high and gradually add the remaining sugar. Continue to whip until stiff peaks form. Gently fold into the custard base until just incorporated. Fold in the candied fruit and rum mixture, then transfer to the prepared crust. Refrigerate until set, about 4 hours.

To finish, in the bowl of a stand mixer fitted with the whisk attachment, whip the cream and icing sugar until stiff peaks form. Transfer the whipped cream to a piping bag fitted with a no. 6 star tip. Pipe a decorative border around the edge, then decorate with candied fruits and marzipan fruits, if using.

Once decorated, this is best eaten straightaway, but it will keep loosely covered in the refrigerator for up to 3 days.

Florentine Tart

In the winter months when one has tired of apples and pears but still craves a chic tart to trot out at their dinner party, this is the answer. Much like the classic cookie, but less finnicky, a crisp buttery crust cradles toasted nuts and candied fruits bound with a salted honey caramel and finished with chocolate. Nothing but praise awaits those who bake this!

Makes one 9-inch tart

---

128 g (6 Tbsp) honey

60 mL (¼ cup) heavy cream

58 g (¼ cup) unsalted butter

50 g (¼ cup) sugar

½ tsp salt

150 g (1½ cups) toasted sliced almonds

65 g (¼ cup) diced candied orange peel (page 33)

65 g (¼ cup) halved candied cherries (page 28 or 33)

50 g (⅓ cup) toasted pistachios

1 tsp vanilla extract

1 fully baked 9-inch Sweet Tart Dough shell (page 198)

45 g (1½ oz) dark chocolate callets

½ tsp neutral oil

To begin, preheat the oven to 350°F (175°C).

In a medium pot over medium-high heat, combine the honey, cream, butter, sugar, and salt. Cook, stirring often, until the mixture turns the color of golden caramel. Remove from the heat and stir in the almonds, candied peel, candied cherries, pistachios, and vanilla.

Place the cooled tart shell on a rimmed baking sheet. Evenly spread the filling in the tart shell.

Bake until the filling is bubbling, about 20 minutes. Cool completely on a wire rack.

To decorate, in a small heatproof bowl, combine the chocolate and oil. Melt over a pot of simmering water or in the microwave in 30-second bursts, stirring often. Drizzle the chocolate over the surface of the tart. Let set before serving.

The tart will keep, covered, at room temperature for up to 5 days.

Old-Fashioned Carrot Pudding

A holiday staple of my childhood, carrot pudding is a kind of poor man's plum pudding, but that's not a bad thing. The carrots bring a subtler sweetness and lighter texture. And don't fear the potato! It will disappear into the mix but help to bind it. Rye flour adds earthiness and mixed citrus adds intrigue. While steaming isn't a common way of cooking desserts in North America, it's wonderful to be able to make this on the stovetop if the oven is busy baking cookies or roasting dinner, though it also freezes admirably if you want to make it in advance.

Serves 8 to 10

---

115 g (½ cup) unsalted butter,
  at room temperature

220 g (1 cup) brown sugar

1 egg

70 g (½ cup) all-purpose flour

70 g (½ cup) rye flour

1½ Tbsp Mixed Spice (page 196)

½ tsp salt

115 g (1 cup) grated carrot

175 g (1 cup) currants

160 g (1 cup) raisins

130 g (½ cup) mixed diced
  candied citrus peel (page 33)

42 g (⅓ cup) slivered almonds

150 g (1 cup) grated peeled
  potato

1 tsp baking soda

1 recipe Custard (page 194),
  for serving

To begin, grease a 7-cup pudding basin (or a stainless-steel bowl or tin can of the same capacity). Fill a large pot, fitted with a steamer large enough to hold your basin, with enough water to reach just under the steamer.

In a large bowl, cream the butter and brown sugar. Beat in the egg, then stir in the all-purpose and rye flours, mixed spice, and salt. Fold in the grated carrot, currants, raisins, candied peel, and slivered almonds.

In a small bowl, combine the grated potato and baking soda. Fold the potato mixture into the pudding mixture. Transfer the batter to the prepared basin and place a round of waxed paper directly on the surface. Cover the basin with foil, then place in the steamer. Cover and bring to a boil over high heat. Reduce the heat to medium and simmer for 3 hours.

To finish, transfer the basin to a wire rack and let cool for 10 minutes. Remove the foil and waxed paper. Use a paring knife to loosen the pudding from the sides of the bowl, then invert agilely onto a serving platter. Serve warm with custard.

Keep any leftovers in an airtight container in the refrigerator for up to 5 days and reheat in the microwave.

Riz a l'Impératrice

This classic French molded rice pudding flavored with kirsch-steeped candied fruits is a showstopper, especially if you use a fun mold and go a little ham on the décor.

Serves 8

125 g (½ cup) mixed diced candied fruits (pages 56–57)

2 Tbsp kirsch

70 g (⅓ cup) short-grain rice, rinsed

688 mL (2¾ cups) whole milk, divided

½ tsp salt

½ vanilla bean, split and scraped

4 egg yolks

75 g (6 Tbsp) sugar

6 g (3 sheets) gelatin, softened

250 mL (1 cup) whipping cream

Candied fruits (pages 56–57), to decorate (optional)

To begin, grease a 6-cup decorative mold with oil. In a small bowl, combine the candied fruits and kirsch.

Bring a medium pot of water to a boil. Add the rice and cook for 2 minutes. Drain and return to the pot, then add 375 mL (1½ cups) milk and the salt. Bring to a simmer over medium heat, then reduce to medium-low and cook, stirring often, until the rice is tender and most of the liquid is absorbed. Transfer to a heatproof bowl.

In a medium pot set over medium heat, combine the remaining milk and vanilla bean. In a medium bowl, whisk yolks with sugar until they lighten a shade. When the milk begins to steam, slowly pour it into the yolk mixture, whisking constantly. Return the mixture to the pot, reduce the heat to medium-low, and cook, stirring constantly, until it reads 180°F (82°C) on an instant-read thermometer or coats the back of a wooden spoon. Stir in the softened gelatin until dissolved, then strain through a fine-mesh sieve into the bowl with the rice. Let the rice mixture cool until barely warm (86°F/30°C), stirring occasionally. Stir in the fruit and kirsch mixture.

To finish, in a medium bowl, whip the cream until firm peaks form. Gently fold into the rice mixture until just incorporated. Transfer to the prepared mold and refrigerate until set, 3 to 4 hours.

To unmold, dip the mold into a bowl of hot water for 5 to 10 seconds, then invert onto a serving dish. Decorate with additional candied fruits, if desired. Leftovers store in an airtight container in the refrigerator for up to 3 days.

FRUITY-FORWARD DESSERTS

White Wine Jelly with Frosted Grapes

A gently gelled mixture of white wine and grape juice garnished with sparkling fresh grapes makes for a light and very sophisticated dessert. You can use whatever dry white wine you like, but if you're not sure, a Riesling would be a good choice. I used a funky dunky natural German white blend, and the jelly tasted like a fragrant Japanese muscat grape candy.

Serves 4

---

250 mL (1 cup) green grape juice

250 mL (1 cup) white wine

50 g (¼ cup) sugar

Pinch of salt

12 g (6 sheets) gelatin, softened

Crystallized grapes (page 49),
   for serving

NOTE *If you can find a high-quality white or green grape juice, wonderful! Otherwise, you can prepare one by simmering grapes with a little water and straining, or using an electric juicer. Probably the easiest is to whizz 370 g (2 cups) grapes in the blender (with a pinch of citric acid or 1 tablespoon lemon juice to help with discoloration), then strain through a fine-mesh sieve. Use a tart-sweet variety, if possible. I like Himrod.*

To begin, grease a 4-cup mold or four ½-cup ramekins lightly with oil.

In a large measuring cup, combine the juice and wine. Measure about 125 mL (½ cup) and place it in a small saucepan. Add the sugar and salt to the saucepan. Heat gently over medium heat until the sugar and salt dissolve. Stir in the gelatin until dissolved. Pour the gelatin mixture back into the juice and wine mixture in the measuring cup and stir to combine. Pour into the mold or divide between the ramekins and refrigerate until set, about 4 hours.

To unmold, dip the mold or ramekins into hot water for 10 seconds. Run a mini offset spatula or paring knife around the edge to loosen, then invert onto a serving platter. Garnish with crystallized grapes and serve immediately.

SIMPLIFY *Omit the crystallized grapes and serve with fresh fruit instead.*

Amaro Blood Oranges

I've seen variations of denuded whole citrus steeped in syrup and garnished with their candied peel. The key is to use excellent fruit, as this is essentially a gussied-up raw orange—a style of dessert I'd like to see more often. This version tempers the sweetness and complements the bitterness of the peel with the addition of Italian amaro. I like to use a blood orange amaro, but anything that plays well with citrus will work—Campari, Montenegro, Vecchio Amaro del Capo . . . Serve this as a winter dessert with some squares of dark chocolate and espresso (or more amaro).

Serves 4 to 6

---

1 kg (2.2 lb) blood oranges

300 g (1½ cups) sugar

1 Tbsp honey

60 mL (¼ cup) amaro

To begin, wash and dry the oranges, then use a vegetable peeler to remove their zest in long strips, leaving behind most of the white pith. Set oranges aside. Make stacks of zest and then julienne crosswise.

In a medium pot set over high heat, bring 500 mL (2 cups) water, sugar, and honey to a boil. Add the julienned zest and reduce the heat to a simmer. Cook until the zest is translucent, 15 to 20 minutes.

Meanwhile, carefully cut all the pith and membranes off the outside of the oranges, leaving them quite bare. Place them in a dish that fits them snugly in a single layer.

When the syrup is ready, remove it from the heat, stir in the amaro, and pour it over the oranges. Leave them to steep at room temperature for at least 4 hours (or overnight, refrigerated), turning them over a few times. Chill for at least 1 hour or up to 5 days before serving.

To serve, place one orange each in shallow serving bowls. Strain the zest, reserving the syrup, and cover each orange entirely with zest so that they look as though they've grown hair. Add a few tablespoons of syrup to each bowl before serving. Serve immediately.

Frozen Yogurt Candied Orange with Aperol Granita

This is a true dream for candied peel lovers—an entire orange all to yourself filled with frozen yogurt (the tarter, the better) and topped with a mountain of sweet-tart orange and Aperol granita.

Serves 6

190 mL (¾ cup) fresh-squeezed orange juice (left over from candied orange shells, page 35)

125 mL (½ cup) Simple Syrup (page 197)

60 mL (¼ cup) Aperol

60 mL (¼ cup) fresh-squeezed lemon juice

6 whole candied orange shells (see variation on page 35), drained and refrigerated

1 pint plain or vanilla frozen yogurt, slightly softened

To begin, make the granita. In a 5 × 9-inch loaf pan, whisk the orange juice, simple syrup, Aperol, and lemon juice. Freeze, whisking every 30 minutes and making sure to scrape the sides, until the mixture is frozen but soft and smooth, 3 to 4 hours total. Cover and keep frozen for up to 2 weeks if not using immediately.

To serve, use a small ice cream scoop to fill the candied orange shells with frozen yogurt, packing it in lightly. Transfer to serving dishes and top with as high a mound of granita as you can manage. Serve immediately.

SIMPLIFY *Omit the candied orange shells; the granita is wonderful on its own. You can also pair it with a contrasting frozen treat like creamy frozen yogurt or vanilla ice cream.*

SUBSTITUTE *No Aperol? Use your favorite amaro or aperitif. No candied orange shells? Use hollowed-out candied lemons, tangerines, or small grapefruit halves (page 35). No frozen yogurt? Use vegan vanilla ice cream or sorbet.*

Pennsylvania Dutch-ish Raisin Fritters

A good fritter is hard to find, but when you do, it's a thing of beauty. A dunk in candied citrus syrup makes these light, yeasty, raisin- and peel-studded donuts super moist, just sweet enough, imbued with flavor, and delightfully glazy.

Makes 9 fritters

---

125 mL (½ cup) buttermilk

280 g (2 cups) all-purpose flour

50 g (¼ cup) sugar

1½ tsp instant yeast

1 tsp salt

58 g (¼ cup) unsalted butter, melted

1 egg

80 g (½ cup) golden raisins

65 g (¼ cup) diced candied peel (page 33)

About 1.5 L (6 cups) canola oil, for frying

250 mL (1 cup) candied citrus syrup (pages 25 or 33)

To begin, in a small saucepan or the microwave for 30 seconds to 1 minute, bring the buttermilk to just warm, 100°F to 110°F (38°C to 43°C). Set aside.

In the bowl of a stand mixer fitted with the dough hook, combine the flour, sugar, yeast, and salt. Add the warmed buttermilk, butter, and egg. Mix on low speed until combined. Increase the speed to medium-low and knead until the dough is smooth and elastic, 5 to 10 minutes. Remove the dough hook and knead in the raisins and candied peel by hand. Cover with a tea towel and let stand for 10 minutes.

Turn the dough out onto a generously floured surface and sprinkle with more flour. Roll or pat into a 9-inch square. Cut into three equal strips both vertically and horizontally, making nine squares. Arrange the squares so they are 1 inch apart, cover them with a tea towel, and let rise somewhere warm until they double in size, 40 minutes to 1 hour. (If your kitchen is cool, the oven with the pilot light on is a good option.) They are ready when you poke the dough with a floured finger and the indent stays. Meanwhile, begin to warm up the oil.

To fry, fill a large, heavy-bottomed pot with about 4 inches of oil. Place over medium-high heat and bring the oil to 350°F (175°C). In a small pot or in a heatproof bowl in the microwave, heat the syrup until warm. Line a wire rack with paper towel.

Fry the donuts in two or three batches, making sure they are not overcrowded, for 2 to 3 minutes per side, until dark golden brown and cooked through. Transfer the donuts to the prepared rack. Let cool for a minute, then dip them into warm syrup for 1 to 2 seconds per side. Return to the wire rack.

Donuts are at their best eaten immediately but will still be very enjoyable at room temperature the day of.

SIMPLIFY *No candied peel? Use extra raisins and the zest of one orange instead. No candied citrus syrup? Use simple syrup (page 197) flavored with the zest and juice of one orange.*

Cassata-ish Semifreddo

This delectable showstopper of a frozen dessert doesn't require an ice cream maker and can be served in a variety of ways. I use a fancy mold and decorate with candied fruits and gold leaf, but you can also simply freeze it in a loaf pan and serve in scoops, with or without the chocolate olive oil magic shell. You might even pipe it into cannoli shells! Or fill sugar cones dipped in the chocolate shell. You've got a lot of really good options. Note: It's best to start this the night before.

Serves 8

150 mL (½ cup + 2 Tbsp) heavy cream

350 g (1⅓ cups) ricotta

2 Tbsp marsala or grappa

Zest of 1 orange

1 tsp vanilla extract

¼ tsp salt

2 eggs

100 g (½ cup) sugar

60 g (3 Tbsp) honey

65 g (¼ cup) diced candied peel (page 33)

40 g (¼ cup) halved candied cherries (pages 28 or 33)

2½ Tbsp toasted pistachios or pine nuts

10 g (⅓ oz) finely grated dark chocolate

175 g (6 oz) dark chocolate pistoles (optional)

To begin, line a 4-cup mold with plastic wrap (or grease with neutral oil, but the semifreddo may be tricky to get out).

In a medium bowl, whip the cream to firm peaks. Refrigerate until ready to use.

In the bowl of a food processor, combine the ricotta, marsala, orange zest, vanilla, and salt. Purée until well combined and the ricotta is smooth.

In a medium heatproof bowl set over a pan of simmering water, combine the eggs, sugar, and honey. Whisk vigorously until the mixture is hot and fluffy and the sugar has dissolved. Remove from the heat and continue to whisk until cool (this is easiest in a stand mixer or using electric beaters!).

Fold the ricotta mixture into the cooled egg mixture until combined. Lighten the mixture by whisking in one-third of the whipped cream, then gently fold in the remaining whipped cream, followed by the candied peel, candied cherries, nuts, and grated chocolate. Scrape into the prepared mold and freeze until solid, at least 5 hours but preferably overnight.

continued

1½ Tbsp extra-virgin olive oil

Candied fruits (pages 56–57),
  to decorate (optional)

Gold leaf, to decorate (optional)

To serve, place in scoops, or unmold by dipping the mold in a bowl of hot water for 10 seconds and then inverting onto a serving plate. Return to the freezer while you prepare the magic shell, if using.

Melt the chocolate pistoles in a medium heatproof bowl set over a pan of simmering water or in the microwave in 30-second increments, stirring between each. Whisk in the oil, then let cool slightly before pouring over the semifreddo.

Decorate with candied fruits and/or gold leaf, if desired, then serve. Keep any leftovers in an airtight container in the freezer for up to 1 week.

SIMPLIFY *Omit the candied peel and use the zest of one extra orange. Use store-bought Amarena cherries instead of homemade.*

Ricotta e Canditi Beignets

The inspiration for these hot little ricotta beignets, studded with candied fruits, chocolate, and pistachios and flavored with a little marsala and espresso, comes from (a) memories of my first pastry assistant job, sneakily making one extra fried-to-order ricotta lemon beignet for myself when that dessert was fired, and (b) one of my favorite gelatos from one of my favorite cookbooks—ricotta e candite from *La Grotta Ices* by Kitty Travers.

Makes 15 beignets

---

260 g (1 cup) whole milk ricotta (preferably sheep's milk)

2 Tbsp sugar

1 Tbsp honey

Zest of ½ lemon

1 egg

1 egg yolk

105 g (¾ cup) all-purpose flour

¼ tsp baking powder

Pinch of salt

1 Tbsp finely chopped dark chocolate

1 Tbsp finely chopped pistachios

1 Tbsp minced candied cherries (page 25 or 28)

1 Tbsp minced candied orange peel (page 33)

½ tsp marsala or grappa

Pinch of ground espresso

About 1.5 L (6 cups) canola oil, for frying

Icing sugar, for dusting

To begin, in a medium bowl, beat the ricotta with the sugar, honey, and lemon zest until smooth. Beat in the egg, followed by the yolk. Mix in the flour, baking powder, and salt just until incorporated. Fold in the chocolate, pistachios, candied cherries and peel, marsala, and espresso. (The batter may be refrigerated, covered, overnight; bring to room temperature before proceeding.)

To fry, fill a large, heavy-bottomed pot with about 4 inches of oil. Place over medium-high heat and bring the oil to 350°F (175°C). Line a wire rack with paper towel. Use a 1 oz (2 tablespoon) scoop to drop the batter into the hot oil. Fry the beignets in two batches for about 5 minutes, reducing the heat if they are browning too quickly, until they are a deep golden brown and cooked through.

Transfer the beignets to the prepared wire rack and use a fine-mesh sieve to dust heavily with icing sugar. Serve immediately.

SIMPLIFY *Omit the candied cherries or peel and use 1 tablespoon minced Amarena or maraschino cherries and the zest of one orange.*

PANTRY STASH

Morning Glory Granola

Years ago at a bakery where I was the pastry chef, I was tasked with creating inventive granola flavors for our retail shelf. It was a no-brainer to create a granola version of our bestselling morning glory muffin, packed with candied carrots and pineapple, currants, pecans, millet, seeds, and spices. I like this best with Greek yogurt for breakfast, but a handful for a snack is never amiss at any hour.

Makes 1.3 kg (3 lb)

490 g (4½ cups) old-fashioned rolled oats

150 g (1¼ cups) pecans

100 g (½ cup) millet

80 g (½ cup) pumpkin seeds

70 g (½ cup) sunflower seeds

60 g (1 cup) unsweetened coconut flakes

2 Tbsp flaxseeds

85 g (¼ cup) liquid honey

60 mL (¼ cup) maple syrup

60 mL (¼ cup) extra-virgin olive oil

58 g (¼ cup) unsalted butter, melted

55 g (¼ cup) brown sugar

¾ tsp five spice powder

¾ tsp salt

100 g (⅔ cup) currants

75 g (⅓ cup packed) dried candied pineapple (page 25), chopped into ½-inch pieces

65 g (½ cup packed) dried candied carrots (page 25)

To begin, preheat the oven to 325°F (160°C). Line a large rimmed baking sheet (or two medium) with parchment paper.

In a large bowl, combine the oats, pecans, millet, pumpkin and sunflower seeds, coconut flakes, and flaxseeds.

In a medium bowl, whisk the honey, maple syrup, oil, melted butter, brown sugar, five spice, and salt. Pour the wet ingredients over the dry ingredients and mix until coated. Spread evenly on the prepared baking sheet.

To bake, place in the oven and stir every 10 minutes, for 20 to 30 minutes, until dry and golden brown. Remove from the oven and place on a wire rack. Scatter with the currants and dried candied pineapple and carrots. Let cool completely before storing in an airtight container. It will keep for at least 1 month.

SIMPLIFY *Omit the candied pineapple or carrots and use store-bought dried or candied pineapple or your favorite dried or candied fruits.*

Caramel Pears

Canned pears are a great staple to put up in the fall, exactly what you need to make gorgeous frangipane tarts and more with ease. These kick it up a notch by caramelizing the sugar for the syrup, imbuing the pears with flavor. They're not candied, but they do have a candied vibe. I like to use citric acid (if I can find it), as it brings fresh fruit acidity back to sweetened, cooked fruit.

Makes three 500 mL (1-pint) jars

300 g (1½ cups) sugar

1 L (4 cups) warm water
   or dry perry

½ tsp citric acid (optional)

¼ tsp salt

1.35 kg (3 lb) pears (about 8,
   such as Bartlett)

Start by making a dry caramel. In a large, heavy-bottomed pot set over medium-high heat, add enough sugar to cover the bottom. Let it melt, undisturbed, until it's a dark amber color. Add more sugar, about 50 g (¼ cup) at a time, stirring it into the caramel until it melts. When all the sugar is incorporated and the caramel is a dark amber, remove from the heat and carefully and gradually add the water. Add the citric acid, if using, and salt. Return the pot to medium heat to dissolve any seized caramel while you prepare the pears.

To prepare the pears, peel, core, and cut the pears into quarters. Add the pears to the pot and heat, stirring occasionally, until they are just warmed through, about 5 minutes. Use a slotted spoon to transfer the pears to clean pint jars, packing them to within ½ inch of the rim. Top with syrup to within ½ inch of the rim, lightly tap the jar to remove any air bubbles, and readjust headspace if necessary. Wipe the rim with a damp, clean paper towel or cloth. Place new snap lids on each jar and seal with ring bands until finger-tip tight (until you just feel resistance).

To heat-process, bring a large pot of water to a boil, covered. Turn off heat. There should be enough water to cover the filled jars by 1 to 2 inches and something on the bottom to protect the jars from the hot metal (e.g., a perforated pizza pan, round cake rack, silicone mat, tea towel . . .).

Place the jars in the water bath, cover, and bring to a boil over high heat. Reduce the heat to medium and set the timer to 20 minutes.

After 20 minutes of heat-processing, turn off heat, remove the lid, and let the jars sit in the water for 5 minutes. Without tipping the jars, transfer them from the pot to a tea towel, wire rack, or wooden board. Allow to sit undisturbed for 24 hours before checking the seals, labeling, and storing somewhere cool, dark, and dry, where they will keep for at least 1 year

Quince & Chestnut Jam

This is the most special jam. You'll want to hide the jars at the back of the pantry and only give them away to your most beloved. Equally at home on a cheeseboard or in a pastry, this stunning coral jam is fragrant with quince and punctuated with bursts of candied chestnut. Note: You will want to start this the night before.

Makes five 250 mL (½-pint) jars

---

1 kg (2.2 lb) quince (about 3–4)

600 g (3 cups) sugar, divided

45 mL (3 Tbsp lemon juice)

1 vanilla bean, split and scraped

85 g (½ cup) diced candied
   chestnuts (pages 28 or 33)

30–45 mL (2–3 Tbsp) brandy
   or rum (optional)

To begin, peel, quarter, and core the quinces, reserving the scraps. Thinly slice crosswise and place in a large, heavy-bottomed pot with 300 g (1½ cups) sugar and 2 L (8 cups) water. Bundle the scraps and place in a cheesecloth or a jelly bag and tie tightly. Add the bundle to the pot. Bring to a boil over high heat.

Reduce the heat to medium and simmer, uncovered, until the quinces are tender and pink (it's okay—desirable even—if some start to break down). This should take about 1 hour. Remove from the heat, cover, and let stand overnight.

The next day, prepare the clean jars by placing them in a preheated 250°F (120°C) oven for at least 20 minutes. Have new snap lids and ring bands at the ready.

Remove the bag of scraps from the pot, squeezing to release all the pectin-rich liquid. Add the remaining sugar, lemon juice, and vanilla bean. Bring to a boil over medium-high heat, then add the candied chestnuts. Boil hard until the setting point is reached. To help determine this, test the set when the bubbles become larger and more rhythmic and start sputtering slightly violently, and the surface of the jam is glossy and jewel-like. The jam should slide off the spatula in

continued

sheets or clumps or try to cling to the spatula when you bring it to eye level. If you're uncertain, put a teaspoon of jam on an ice-cold plate and place in the freezer for 2 minutes. Remove and run your finger through the jam. If it has formed a skin and parts evenly, it's ready; if not, continue cooking a few minutes longer and try again.

Add the brandy, if using. Ladle into the prepared jars to within ¼ to ⅛ inch of the rim. Lightly tap the jar to remove any air bubbles, wipe the rims with a damp paper towel if necessary, top with new snap lids, seal tightly with ring bands, and invert for 1 to 2 minutes.

Flip the jars right side up and allow them to cool for 24 hours. Check the seals before storing somewhere cool, dark, and dry, where the jam will keep for at least 1 year.

SIMPLIFY *Omit the candied chestnuts.*

SUBSTITUTE *No candied chestnuts? Use candied cranberries (page 39) or diced candied orange (page 25).*

Raspberry–Yuzu Jam

Tart raspberries and fragrant candied yuzu peel are a match made in heaven, perfect for enjoying with a croissant or flavoring a Japanese-style cream roll.

Makes four 250 mL (½-pint) jars

1.2 kg (9½ cups) raspberries
(fresh or frozen)

600 g (3 cups) sugar

60 mL (¼ cup) yuzu juice

70 g (¼ cup) chopped candied
yuzu peel (pages 28 or 33)

SUBSTITUTE *No yuzu juice or candied yuzu peel? Use lemon juice and mixed candied peel (page 33) and add two whole star anise at the beginning of cooking (remove before jarring).*

Recipe pictured on page 186

To begin, in a bowl, combine the raspberries, sugar, and yuzu juice. Let macerate for at least 15 minutes or up to 1 week, covered, in the refrigerator.

Prepare the clean jars by placing them in a preheated 250°F (120°C) oven for at least 20 minutes. Have new snap lids and ring bands at the ready.

Transfer the macerated fruit to a wide, heavy-bottomed pot and add the candied yuzu peel. Bring to a hard boil, stirring frequently, until the setting point is reached. To help determine this, test the set when the bubbles become larger and more rhythmic and start sputtering slightly violently, and the surface of the jam is glossy and jewel-like. The jam should slide off the spatula in sheets or clumps or try to cling to the spatula when you bring it to eye level. If you're uncertain, put a teaspoon of jam on an ice-cold plate and place in the freezer for 2 minutes. Remove and run your finger through the jam. If it has formed a skin and parts evenly, it's ready; if not, continue cooking a few minutes longer and try again.

To finish, remove from the heat and ladle into a heatproof measuring jug. Pour into the prepared jars to within ¼ to ⅛ inch of the rim. Wipe the rims with a damp paper towel, if necessary, top with new snap lids, seal tightly with ring bands, and invert for 1 to 2 minutes.

Flip the jars right side up and allow them to cool for 24 hours. Check the seals before storing somewhere cool, dark, and dry, where the jam will keep for at least 1 year.

Raspberry-Yuzu Jam (page 185)

Manhattan Cherries

I love a Manhattan—whisky, sweet vermouth, orange bitters, and a cherry. These cherries are a garnish but also contain all the flavors of the cocktail in one bite, stuffed with candied orange peel and steeped in liquor. If you use them to garnish a Manhattan, that's a Manhattan squared! The infinity mirror of drinks. This doubles (or triples!) admirably, and you can also divide it between smaller jars for gifting.

Makes about one 500 mL (1-pint) jar

About 350 g (2 cups) dark, sweet cherries

50 g candied orange peel (page 28 or 33)

About 90 mL (6 Tbsp) sweet red vermouth

About 90 mL (6 Tbsp) rye or bourbon

¼ tsp orange bitters

To begin, pit the cherries, preferably with a cherry pitter, which will do the job cleanly. Leave the stems on.

Cut the candied peel into ¼-inch strips, then cut those strips into 1-inch pieces. Stuff a piece of peel into each cherry, then pack them into the jar.

To finish, in a measuring cup, combine the vermouth, rye, and bitters. Add the vermouth mixture to the jar to cover the cherries (you might need a few tablespoons more of each). Close tightly with a clean lid and let sit at room temperature, in a cool spot, for 2 weeks, turning the jar a few times whenever you think of it. Transfer to the refrigerator, where cherries will keep for at least 1 year.

BASE
RECIPES

Brown Butter

I like to make a large amount of brown butter at a time, rather than browning it for each recipe I want to use it in. If you have any left over, try using it on vegetables or instead of oil for a vinaigrette.

Makes 400 g (1¾ cups)

---

454 g (1 lb) unsalted butter

Have a heatproof container at the ready.

Cut the butter into chunks and place in a medium saucepan. Melt over medium-high heat and continue to cook until the foam subsides and the butter smells like toffee and toasted nuts. (Keep an eye on it, as it can burn quickly.) There will be brown caramelized milk solids on the bottom of the pan.

Immediately remove from the heat and transfer to the heatproof container. Allow to cool to room temperature before using or refrigerating for future use.

The butter will keep in an airtight container in the refrigerator for up to 2 weeks.

Caramel

I learned to make this caramel from the most talented confiseuse I know, Catherine Lepine Lafrance. She once owned a shop called Dinette Nationale in Montreal, where she candied all sorts of fruits and made caramel spreads in myriad flavors. This is an ingredient in the Pear, Hazelnut & Caramel Layer Cake (page 97), but it's good to have some on hand at all times, if you ask me. Heated and thinned out with a little cream, it makes an excellent caramel sauce.

Makes 500 g (2 cups)

---

375 mL (1½ cups) whipping cream

½ vanilla bean, split and scraped

250 g (1¼ cups) sugar

115 g (½ cup) unsalted butter, cubed

1 tsp flaky salt

In a small pot set over medium-low heat, combine the cream and vanilla bean.

Meanwhile, prepare a dry caramel by placing a medium pot over medium-high heat. Add enough sugar to cover the bottom of the pot and wait (don't stir it!) until it liquefies and turns amber. Pour in about 50 g (¼ cup) sugar. Once this has dissolved and caramelized, add the same amount again. When all the sugar has dissolved and is a nice dark amber color, remove from the heat and carefully stir in the hot cream little by little.

Return the pot to the stove and cook, stirring occasionally, until a thermometer inserted into the mixture reads 223°F (106°C). Add the butter and salt and stir until incorporated. Transfer to a heatproof container and let cool to room temperature before using. It will keep in the refrigerator for up to 1 month.

Custard

If I had my druthers, I'd pour custard on almost everything. I realize that's not reasonable, but you MUST pour it on Old-Fashioned Carrot Pudding (page 156) at the very least. It's also excellent on fruit crumbles and all manner of steamed puddings.

Makes 560 mL (2¼ cups)

500 mL (2 cups) heavy cream

5 egg yolks

50 g (¼ cup) sugar

2¼ tsp cornstarch

2½ tsp vanilla extract

In a medium pot over medium heat, begin to heat the cream. Meanwhile, in a medium bowl, whisk the yolks, sugar, and cornstarch together until the mixture becomes a few shades paler.

When the cream starts to simmer, pour it gradually into the yolk mixture, whisking constantly. Return the mixture to the pot and cook over medium-low heat, stirring constantly, until the custard coats a wooden spoon. Remove from the heat and stir in the vanilla.

Serve immediately or store in an airtight container in the refrigerator for up to 3 days. Reheat gently on the stove or in the microwave.

VARIATION *Use 2 tablespoons brandy or dark rum for the vanilla.*

Custard Buttercream

This buttercream changed my life. It tastes like vanilla ice cream (though takes on flavor very well), isn't too sweet, has a gorgeous texture, and freezes well. What more could you want in a buttercream? It's my signature cake companion—and maybe now it's yours too!

Makes 570 g (3 cups)

250 mL (1 cup) heavy cream

1 egg yolk

2 tsp vanilla extract

1½ tsp cornstarch

230 g (1 cup) unsalted butter, at room temperature

125 g (1 cup) icing sugar

Pinch of salt

In a small pot, whisk the cream, yolk, vanilla, and cornstarch. Bring to a gentle boil over medium heat, stirring constantly.

Strain the mixture through a fine-mesh sieve into the bowl of a stand mixer. Fit the mixer with the whisk attachment and whip the mixture on high speed until cool.

Add the butter, icing sugar, and salt and mix on medium-low speed until incorporated. Increase the speed to medium-high and whip until the buttercream is smooth and silky.

Use immediately or freeze in an airtight container for up to 3 months. Let it come to room temperature before rewhipping.

Mixed Spice

It's been over a decade now since I came up with this blend, which is perfect for bringing winter warmth and holiday spirit to anything it touches.

Makes 60 mL (¼ cup)

---

2 tsp whole cloves

6 allspice berries

1 star anise

3 green cardamom pods
   (husks discarded)

3 blades of mace (optional)

1 Tbsp + 1 tsp cinnamon

1½ tsp ground ginger

1 tsp freshly grated nutmeg

Use a spice grinder (mine doubles as my coffee grinder!) to finely grind the cloves, allspice, star anise, cardamom seeds, and mace, if using. Transfer to a small jar and mix in the cinnamon, ginger, and nutmeg.

The spice will keep in a tightly sealed jar at room temperature for at least 6 months.

Simple Syrup

This versatile building block couldn't be easier to make and is easy to scale up or down. I almost always have some on hand—mostly for cocktails but also for making a quick batch of Candied Fruit Lite (page 43). That said, once you have a surplus of candied fruit syrup on hand, it can easily sub in for simple syrup in many cocktail recipes or other uses such as moistening cake layers. It's also easy to flavor simple syrup—add citrus zest, herbs, or even tea or coffee; strain once the infusion is at your desired strength.

Makes 375 mL (1½ cups)

---

200 g (1 cup) sugar

Flavor of choice (zest, herbs, tea, coffee, etc.)

In a small pot, combine the sugar with 250 mL (1 cup) water. Bring to a boil over medium-high heat, stirring occasionally. Continue to boil until sugar has dissolved, about 30 seconds. Add the desired flavor and let steep to taste. Strain if necessary, then transfer syrup to a heatproof container and let cool completely before refrigerating. The syrup will keep for up to 1 month.

VARIATION *For sugar syrup, simply double the sugar.*

Sweet Tart Dough

This makes a gorgeous, crisp, cookie-like crust. The warmer the dough, though, the more difficult it is to handle, so just let it temper enough that you can roll it and no more. That said, if all else fails, you can just press it into the tart pan as evenly as possible.

Makes one 9-inch tart shell

185 g (¾ cup + 1 Tbsp) softened unsalted butter

42 g (⅓ cup) icing sugar

¼ tsp salt

210 g (1½ cups) all-purpose flour

4 tsp heavy cream

In the bowl of a stand mixer fitted with the paddle attachment, beat the butter, icing sugar, and salt on medium speed until well combined and fluffy. Add the flour and mix on low until it's mostly incorporated. Add the cream and mix on low until the dough comes together.

On a lightly floured work surface, turn out the dough and smoosh it a few times with the heel of your hand to really make it homogeneous—no corner should be crumbly or dry. Form the dough into a disk, wrap it in plastic, and refrigerate for at least 1 hour or up to 3 days. (Or freeze it for up to 2 months. Thaw it in the refrigerator and bring to room temperature before using.)

To fully bake, let the dough rest at room temperature for 15 minutes. Grease a 9-inch tart pan, then roll out the dough to ⅛ inch thick. Either roll it up on your rolling pin and unroll it over the pan or fold it into quarters and unfold it in the pan. Use a pastry brush to dust off any excess flour as you go. Snuggle the dough into the sides of the pan and trim the edges flush with the sides. Refrigerate for at least 30 minutes or up to overnight.

When ready to bake, preheat the oven to 375°F (190°C). Dock the dough by piercing it repeatedly with a fork over the bottom and side. Line the tart shell with heavy-duty plastic wrap, then fill with pie weights or dried beans. Bake for 20 minutes, carefully remove the plastic wrap and pie weights and bake for 10 minutes, until the entire crust is golden brown. Allow to cool completely before using.

Acknowledgments

I am immensely grateful!

For everyone who has attended my candied fruit workshops—this book wouldn't exist if you weren't all so psyched to candy fruit.

To Stonesong Literary Agency, for supporting and advocating for me throughout this process.

To Robert McCullough; my wonderful editor, Katherine Stopa; and the whole team at Appetite.

To my favorite photographer, Mickaël Bandassak, for your brilliant work and for giving us an excuse to come to Paris.

To Michelle Marek: stylist, pastry chef, and friend beyond compare—I never want to work without you! Thanks for the excellent recipes too.

To Tim Mazurek, a beautiful person and writer. I couldn't ask for a better fruit foreworder.

To Chi Nguyễn, Bronwen Wyatt, David Courteau, Catherine Roberge, Giselle Courteau, and Catherine Lepine Lafrance, friends and constant pastry inspirations, for lending me your brilliant recipes and techniques.

To Blake Mackay & Take Care Studio for a home away from home in Montreal and the best props.

To Cafe Verlet & David Hernandez for welcoming us into their beautiful space and letting us interrupt afternoon teatime.

To my most helpful and lovely aunts, Susan, Sandra, and Lorna, for helping track down beloved childhood recipes.

To Winnie Lem and Gavin Smith—we couldn't have gone to Paris without your generosity!

To Fraser & Aldergrove Farm for growing fresh ginger (and all the other best food).

To Hailey McCron for finding a giant pile of fresh hibiscus, candying them, and sharing with me.

And for the first time, I'm honored to thank my crack team of recipe testers, who have made the recipes in this book so much better. JoMarie Ricketts, Karen Huff, Kathryn McClelland, Bronwen Wyatt (again!), Tim Mazurek (again!), Alex Smith, Susannah Lescher, Grace Parker, Hallie Sharpless, Rebecca Carpenter, Anya Kurennaya, Katie Stelmanis, Sarah Eden, Cora Loechler, In Chieh Chen, April McGreger, Chi Nguyễn (again!), Sarah Pierce, and Kelly Bennett Heyd—you are all ANGELS.

Always, saving the best for last, to Kat and Dorian, my loves, for making my life infinitely better.

Bibliography

Davidson, Alan. *The Penguin Companion to Food*. London: Penguin Paperbacks, 2004.

Greweling, Peter P. *Chocolates and Confections: Formula, Theory, and Technique for the Artisan Confectioner*. Hoboken: Wiley, 2012.

Hood, Sarah B. *Jam, Jelly and Marmalade: A Global History*. London: Reaktion Books, 2021.

Larousse Librairie. *Larousse Gastronomique: The World's Greatest Culinary Encyclopedia*. New York City: Clarkson Potter, 2009.

McGee, Harold. *On Food and Cooking: The Science and Lore of the Kitchen*. New York City: Scribner, 2004.

Shephard, Sue. *Pickled, Potted, and Canned: How the Art and Science of Food Preserving Changed the World*. New York City: Simon & Schuster, 2006.

Index